Vintage Grain

The Mitzvah of Keeping Yashan

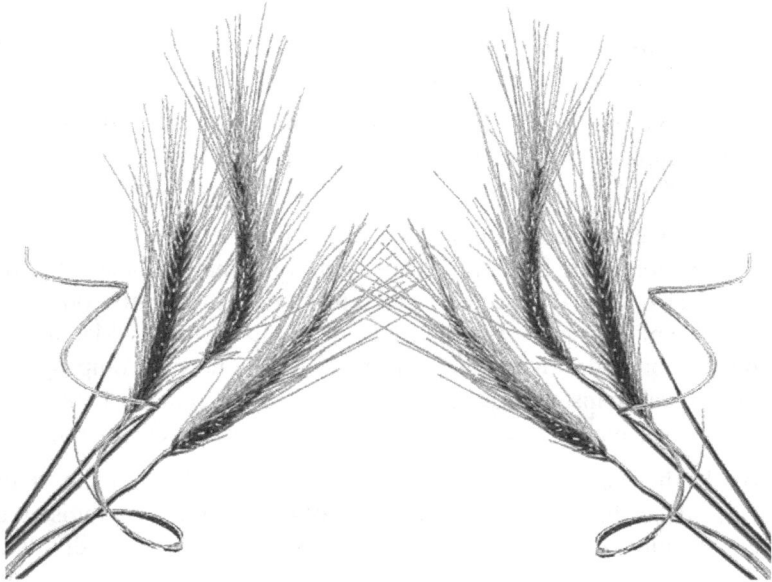

Chasya Katriela Eshkol

Vintage Grain: The Mitzvah of Keeping Yashan

Library of Congress Control Number: 2017915045

ISBN: 978-0-9994786-9-1

Published by Tovim Press LLC.
TovimPress.com

VintageGrainBook.com

Rabbi Zev Leff

Rabbi of Moshav Matityahu
Rosh HaYeshiva—Yeshiva Gedola Matityahu

הרב זאב לף

מרא דאתרא מושב מתתיהו
ראש הישיבה—ישיבה גדולה מתתיהו

Dear Friends,

I have seen the book "Vintage Grain" by Chasya Katriela Eshkol. The book presents a comprehensive discussion of the prohibition of chodosh – new grain that grows before Pesach and is prohibited until the second day of Pesach. The book explains the prohibition and extensively gives advice on how to identify products that present an issue of chodosh and how to identify products that are yashan and are therefore permissable.

Although the prevailing custom is to permit chodosh on grains grown outside of Eretz Yisroel especially in non-Jewish owned fields (as mentioned in the book on page 51) however many opinions prohibit chodosh even in such grain and more and more people are accepting this strigency and are careful to only eat products that are yashon.

This book covers the issues involved and presents many interesting facts about the food industry and its history. I found this book informative, interesting and even entertaining. I recommend it not only to those who are stringent concerning yashan, but even to those who do not adhere to this stringency, but should be aware of the issue and be well informed of a Torah mitzvah that at least applies even today in Eretz Yisroel.

I pray that Hashem bless the authoress with life and health and commend her for a quality presentation that merits the community.

Sincerely,
With Torah blessings

Rabbi Zev Leff

This Book is Lovingly Dedicated

to my wonderful husband

Shmaryahu Jaim Eshkol, who inspires

me to always grow and improve.

Vintage Grain

The Mitzvah of Keeping Yashan

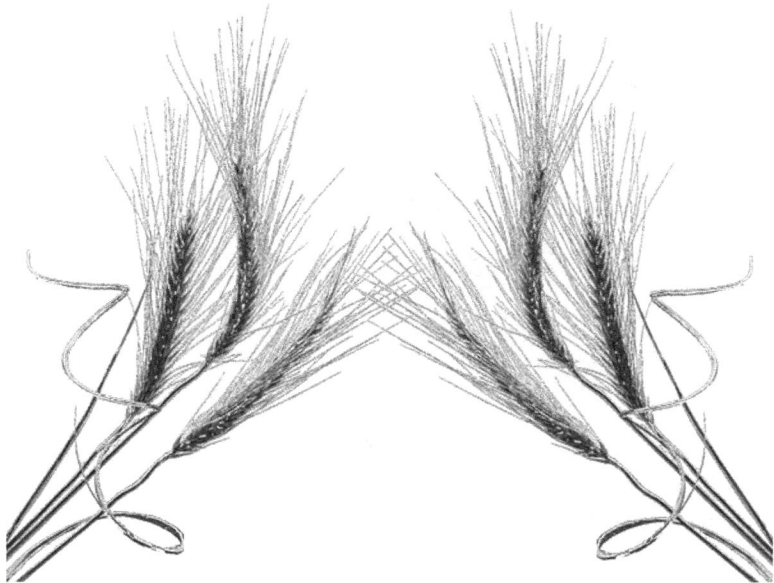

Chasya Katriela Eshkol

Tovim Press

book publishing services that are simply, Tov!

Published by Tovim Press, LLC.

This Paperback version would not be complete without mention of the passing of Rabbi Yoseph Herman zt"l, a few months ago. May his holy work continue to thrive and prosper through Project Chodosh, the organization he created. He inspired so many people including this author, with his tireless work and incredible modesty. May this book be a merit to his memory, and aid in continuing his quest of helping others to keep the mitzvah of yashan.

Table of Contents

Chapter 2 ~ Foods for Thought

Chapter 3 ~ Is It Realistic?

Chapter 4 ~ History of Packaged Foods

Chapter 5 ~ Determining Yashan Status

Chapter 6 ~ Diving into Vintage Grain

Chapter 7 ~ "I Like My Noodles Old!"

Resources

External Yashan Resources

Vintage Grain Reference Resources

Introduction

"So, what exactly is *yashan*?", people often ask me. This is not always a simple question to answer. Although my husband says I should learn to answer this question within one sentence, I'm not quite sure that is quite possible.

Far too often, when people hear the translation of "yashan", meaning "old" or specifically "old grain", it sounds like stale food. If you think about it, back in the days of the Temple, it was just another commandment that people kept. They didn't have processing and preservatives. If the Torah said something was good for us, you listened! After all, what is it that makes gourmet basmati rice so special? It is aged! Just like fine wine and seasoned condiments, grain can get better with age as well. To preserve them, one must treat *yashan* items carefully, but with today's technology it is easy. One simply has to learn how to go about it.

Years ago, when I first took upon the *mitzvah* [law] of "Keeping Yashan", I would quietly say under my breath to my hosts, "Umm, yes, I keep *yashan*, and can only eat certain things." Nowadays, with so many health issues, dietary restrictions, and allergies, it's usually not a problem. "Gluten-free" is now a common, everyday term. Instead of saying, "I keep *yashan* which means old grain", perhaps a better phrase to say is, "I eat "vintage grain". How dignified!

The all too often "dry" topic of keeping *yashan* can be a bit involved. Therefore, the material presented in this book will ideally help to instill the ideas of "how" and "why", with as much explanation and as little confusion as possible for the newcomer. Noting the growing number of zealous *gerim* [converts] and *ba'alei teshuvot* [Jews returning to Torah observance], I use the *Sefardic* or modern Israeli Hebrew, as most (including myself) are more familiar with it. Many of us didn't grow up with "Yeshivish" and Yiddish terms appearing in many articles on *kashrut* [pertaining to kosher] and the *Guide to Chodosh* (the *yashan*-keeping "bible"). This book is also ideal for anyone in the kosher food service industry who would like to cater to Israelis or a larger Jewish clientele.

I endeavor to allow all people to be able to understand the concepts and terms presented. To help remedy this, at the first mention of Hebrew words or terms, there is a definition in brackets, so that the general newcomer can learn and understand them. My wish is to enable them to fulfill the *mitzvah* with confidence, complete understanding, and ease. There is also a glossary provided in the back.

It is my hope to provide an "easy read", that's informative yet entertaining, in printed format that can be read any time. Full of beautiful color photographs, it is sure to help educate and provide enjoyment at the same time. One can even sit back and have fun reading it on *Shabbat*.

For those who like to look at things from a scholarly point of view, the concept of grain getting better with age is actually backed up by Rashi in his commentary on *Vayikra* [Leviticus] 26:10, concerning the *Yovel* [Jubilee] year and the *Sh'mittah* [sabbatical year] crops. It is also supported by the sages of the *Talmud* in *Bava Batra* 91b. Concerning the blessings if we follow Hashem's laws, it is said that the crops will be in such abundance, that we will eat very old (*yashan*) grain and we will have to move out the old (*yashan*) to make room for the *chadash* [new grain]. (*Chadash* is also spelled "chodosh" in *Ashkenazi* [Eastern European] Hebrew.) The commentators reiterate how this aged "vintage grain" will be far superior in quality to the newer grain, and how it indeed improves with age.

Whether you just want to learn more, or you would like to take the plunge into this *mitzvah*, "Vintage Grain" is for you. It tells you everything you need to know, from how and when to start keeping the *mitzvah*, to knowing what is *yashan* nearly at a glance. (Well, nearly!) Being a beginner can be a bit tricky at first, but once you learn about it, it is easy. With tips, charts, resources and lists, you too can "reap" the benefits of *Vintage Grain*.

—— Chasya Katriela Eshkol

Acknowledgments

It is with extreme gratitude to *Hashem Yitbarach* [our Creator, may He be blessed] that I am able to compile this book on one of His lesser-known *mitzvot* [laws]. I can only hope that I can do it justice. It's my ambition to help make a seemingly complex law become a reality for those who truly want to keep this *mitzvah*.

A word of appreciation to those associated with The Yoshon Network Inc. (TYNI), for making our non-profit organization a reality! *Todah Rabbah* to fellow directors Rabbi Avrohom Weinrib and Mrs. Leah Newmark, and our registered agent Mr. Shmuel "Paul" Plotsker, Esq. With their help, wisdom and advice, TYNI has been able to reach thousands of people around the world with our website "Yoshon.com". TYNI would not exist without them!

I must thank my husband Shmaryahu Jaim Eshkol, for all his patience and donating his valuable time and resources for the cause of keeping *yashan*. He deserves extra praise for his vision, plus designing and building the beautiful, functional, user-friendly Yoshon.com website we have today. Always striving for improvement, without his encouragement, this book quite possibly may not have ever been written.

These Acknowledgements would not be complete without mention of Rabbi Yoseph Herman [z"l], and his assistant Mrs. Chaya Rosskamm for their pioneering work through Project Chodosh Inc. Although not affiliated with TYNI or Yoshon.com in the slightest, they have answered numerous *yashan* questions of mine. I am truly indebted to them and their tireless work. It has been such an inspiration to me. Their efforts are to be applauded! I thank Rabbi Herman for offering excellent advice.

Sincere appreciation to Rabbi Moshe Reich of Kof-K for taking his valuable time to explain many *yashan* issues to me, and for his kind words. Much gratitude to Rabbi David Spetner, Rosh Kollel of the Cincinnati Community Kollel who helped guide me with sources, and for contacting Rav Moshe Heinemann of Star-K on my behalf to clarify an issue. A special "Thank You" to Rabbi Pinchas G. Allouche and Rabbi Melech Berlove for assisting with source translations. Also, a word of thanks to Rabbi David Gorelik of OU for helping elucidate the sprouted grain issue.

A special note of gratitude to Rabbi Yaakov Lustig z"l, for information on his teacher Rabbi Eliezer Silver z"l.

With this book and the help of those mentioned, (and those who wished to remain anonymous), it is my hope to put the *mitzvah* of keeping *yashan* in these complex times of modern food manufacturing within every Jew's grasp.

"Gluten-Free" Products may not be
"Five-Grain-Free", and contain Oats!
(See pages 27-28.)

Beer made with Barley Malt.
(More on pages 88-89.)

Multigrain Cereals and
other "Multigrain"
Products may or may
not contain the
Five Grains!
(See page 28.)

Chapter 1

Be Bold, Go "Old"?

What Is Yashan? *Yashan* (also spelled "yoshon" in *Ashkenazi* Hebrew) is defined as "old grain". No, it is not at all stale food! We will take an in-depth look at this *mitzvah*.

First, let's look at the sources, for the scholarly among us who like to know how the *mitzvah* [law] originated. In our context, it is referred to as "the *mitzvah* of keeping *yashan*". The actual law is often referred to as "the prohibition of eating *chadash*" [new grain], and is based on three separate negative commandments according to the Rambam's 613 *mitzvot* [laws]. Interestingly, the prohibition of eating *chametz* [leavened] items during *Pesach* [Passover] is only one negative commandment!

Yashan is derived from the Torah in *Vayikra* [Leviticus] 23:14. Simply put, one can't eat grain within the same yearly cycle in which it was rooted. In the *Talmud, Menachot* 70a, it's mentioned in the *Mishnah* and expounded upon in the *Gemarah*.

"Yashan" (referring to grain) is found in the Torah four times, and "chadash" (for grain) is only found once, and within the same sentence as *Yashan*. It's known that the Torah repeats an item to emphasize its importance.

7

How Did Yashan Originate?

The *Omer* offering of barley was brought to the *Beit HaMikdash* [the Temple] starting on the second day of *Pesach.* Barley was the first crop to ripen, and a measure of one "Omer" (around 8-9 cups) was brought each day. Today, without the Temple, the *Omer* is counted verbally until the holiday of *Shavuot*, and not with physical barley. However, even now that special "second day of *Pesach*" remains a marker for *yashan.* Grain plants and their seeds (and products made from them) that rooted before that day are permissible to eat from then on. They are considered *yashan* or "old", as they existed on or before that day. This is expounded upon in the *Talmud, Mishna* 1:1 in *Challah.*

A "New Year" for Grain

The 16th of Nissan is a general milestone for *yashan* and *chadash.* Once *chadash* has gone through a whole year and reached the second day of *Pesach*, it's considered *yashan.* That same date can be considered the "birthday" of *chadash* grain, as any seed that takes root after that day becomes *chadash.* This is what we're prohibited to eat, as it's considered a whole new "entity". Any food made from this grain would also be forbidden until the 16th of Nissan the following year. (Outside of Israel, it is the 17th.) No matter where you are, every product is *yashan* on the first day of *Chol HaMoed* [the in-between days of] *Pesach*!

There are two views as to how long it takes for seeds to sprout. Most rabbis hold that the sowing had to be three days before the second day of *Pesach* (by the 13th of Nissan), but stricter rabbis hold that plants must have been sown two weeks prior, on the 2nd of Nissan! Nonetheless, the USDA provides crop data, and *mashgichim* [kosher supervisors] in charge of checking *yashan* status have to tend to this so we don't need to worry about it except for checking date codes.

ᏮᏣᏮᏣ

What Are the Yashan Grains?

There are Seven Species for which Israel is praised, as mentioned in *Devarim* [Deuteronomy] 8:8. In order: wheat, barley, grapes, figs, pomegranates, olives and dates. You may notice that five of these are fruits- ענבים "anavim" (grapes), תאנה "te'enah" (fig), רימון "rimmon" (pomegranate), זית "zayit" (olive), and תמר "tamar" (date). Only two actual grains, "wheat and barley" are mentioned, which come first in the list, generally denoting importance. That is accurate since grain was one's major sustenance.

As with many other Torah laws, (such as *challah*, *chametz*, and *brachot* for food), *yashan* applies only to the *Chameshet Minei Dagan* [the Five Species of Grain].

They're generally translated as follows: חיטים "chittim" (wheat), שעורים "se'orim" (barley), כוסמין "kusmin" or כוסמת "kusemet" (spelt), שיפון "shifon" (rye), and שיבולת שועל "shibbolet shu'al" (oats). Exactly how do we get five when only two are initially mentioned in the Torah as pertaining to Israel? Wheat and barley are mentioned in the in *Devarim* 8:8 pertaining to *Eretz Yisrael* [the Land of Israel], as well as multiple other times. Spelt is first mentioned in *Shemot* [Exodus] 9:32, but only as being an Egyptian crop that didn't get destroyed in the plague of hail. We see that the Five Grains are not specifically mentioned in the Torah itself. The actual *Chameshet Minei Dagan* are derived from the *Talmud* in *Mishnah, Menachot* 70b.

In putting together this book, I thought it would be interesting to show pictures of the different crops. In a world where a majority of Jews live in the city, it can be hard to relate to the physically growing grain when we can merely open up a package of our favorite food. We have lost sight of the agrarian attitude to be solely dependent on Hashem. The pictures of grains at each stage they go through can help cement that idea. Especially when we see just where it starts, how it grows, what it looks like before harvest, the actual dry grains, and many final products made from them. It's the whole life-cycle of the grains, from field to food.

Let's examine the plants that make up the Five Grains...

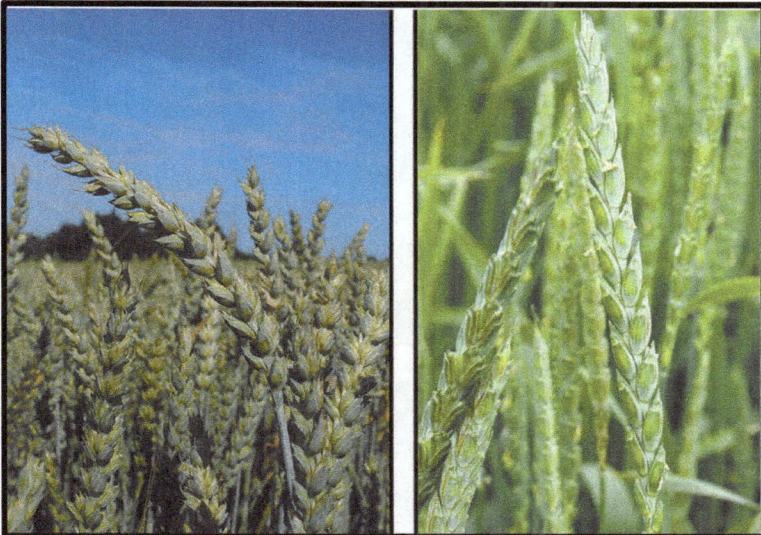

Closely related species, wheat (left) and spelt (right).

Barley

Rye (top) and oats (bottom).

As I proceeded to gather photographs, I noticed just how different the oats looked from the other four species. Now, the beauty of Judaism is that one is encouraged to ask questions, rather than to "take it on faith" like other religions. With this in mind, I decided to investigate. I've always thought that there's no contradiction between science and Torah. It may be a matter of interpretation or what Hashem allows us to perceive. Obviously, being a Torah-related *mitzvah*, I looked into sources from *Halacha* [Jewish law]. To further back things up, I also looked into the scientific aspects of the *Chameshet Minei Dagan*, and it was amazing what I found!

A closeup of Barley (above) and Oats (below) reveals how dissimilar they really are.

This issue will be explored later in detail. For now, we will look at where the Five Grains originally came from.

Let's see a "Family Tree" of the world grains…

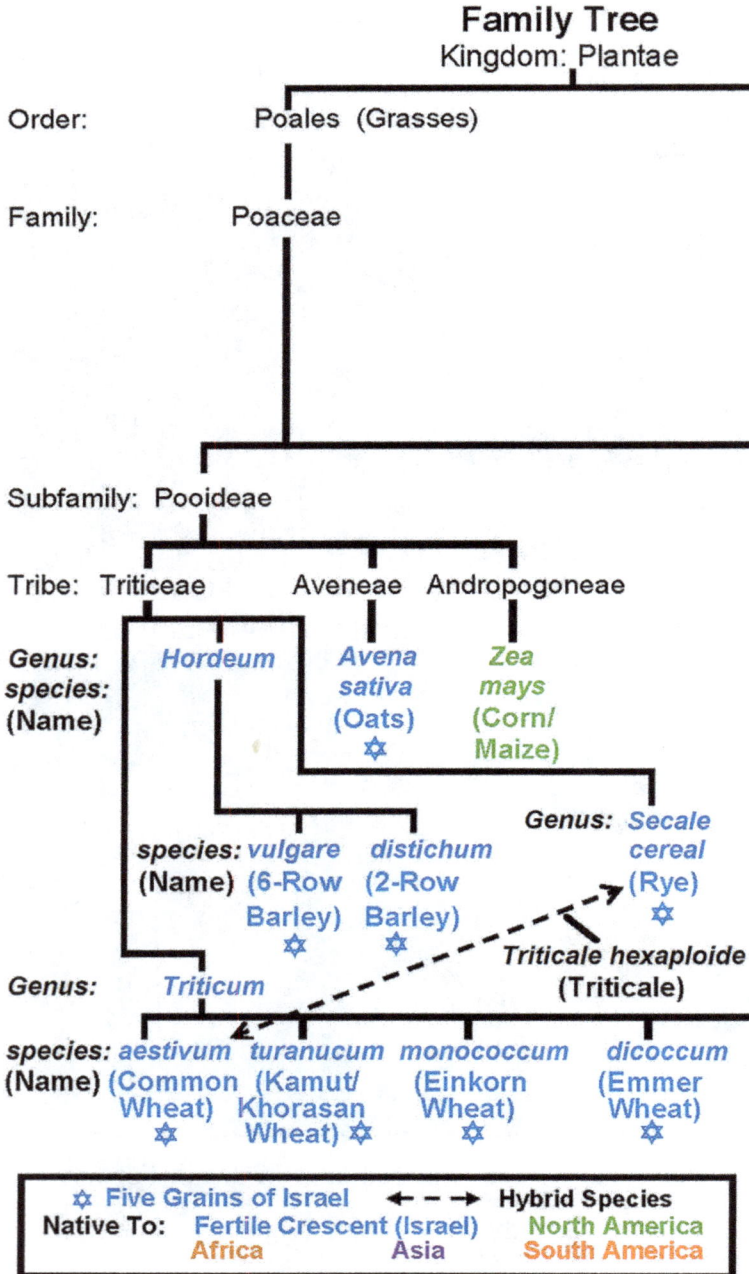

Family Tree
Kingdom: Plantae

Order: Poales (Grasses)

Family: Poaceae

Subfamily: Pooideae

Tribe: Triticeae Aveneae Andropogoneae

Genus:
species:
(Name)

Hordeum *Avena sativa* (Oats) ✡ *Zea mays* (Corn/ Maize)

Genus: *Secale cereal* (Rye) ✡

species:
(Name)

vulgare (6-Row Barley) ✡ *distichum* (2-Row Barley) ✡

Triticale hexaploide (Triticale)

Genus: *Triticum*

species:
(Name)

aestivum (Common Wheat) ✡ *turanucum* (Kamut/ Khorasan Wheat) ✡ *monococcum* (Einkorn Wheat) ✡ *dicoccum* (Emmer Wheat) ✡

✡ **Five Grains of Israel** ← – → **Hybrid Species**
Native To: **Fertile Crescent (Israel)** **North America**
Africa **Asia** **South America**

14

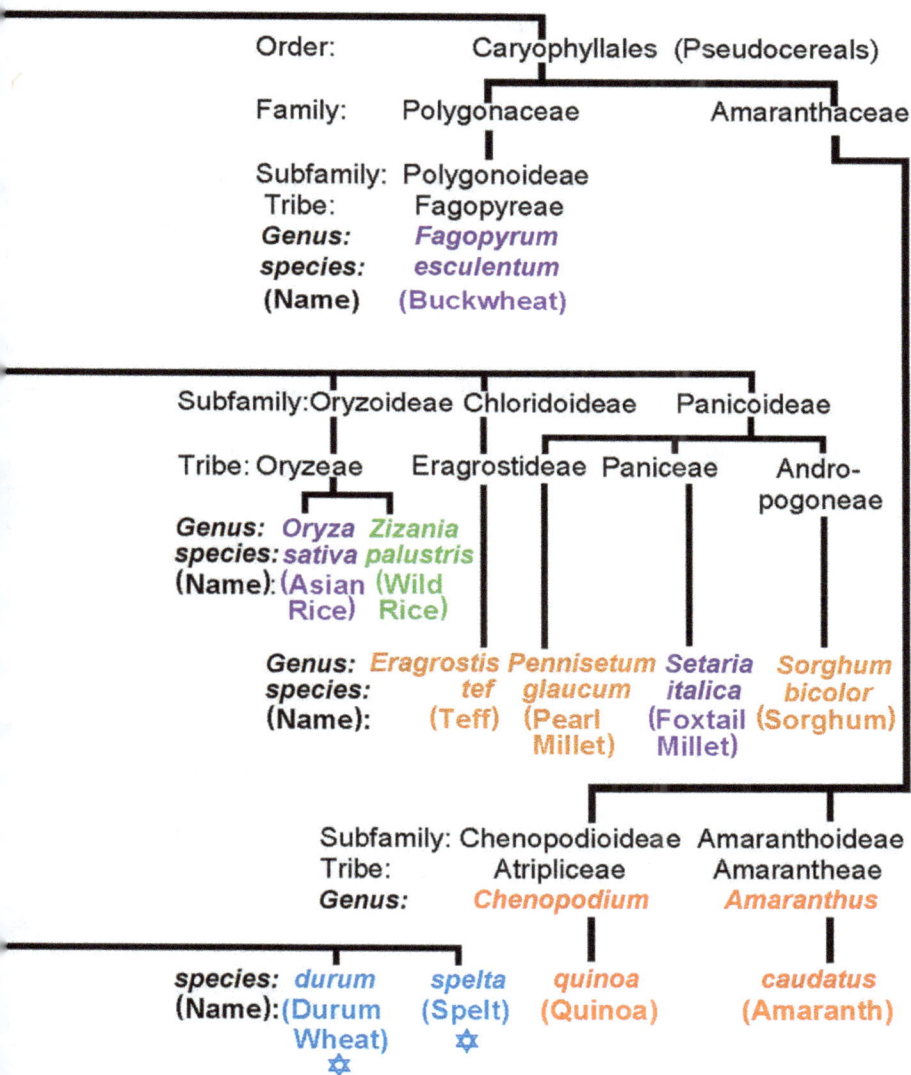

Order: Caryophyllales (Pseudocereals)

Family: Polygonaceae   Amaranthaceae

Subfamily: Polygonoideae
Tribe: Fagopyreae
Genus: *Fagopyrum*
species: *esculentum*
(Name)   **(Buckwheat)**

Subfamily: Oryzoideae Chloridoideae Panicoideae

Tribe: Oryzeae   Eragrostideae Paniceae Andro-
                                                       pogoneae

Genus: *Oryza* *Zizania*
species: *sativa* *palustris*
(Name): (Asian (Wild
              Rice) Rice)

Genus: *Eragrostis* *Pennisetum* *Setaria*   *Sorghum*
species: *tef*   *glaucum*   *italica*   *bicolor*
(Name):   (Teff)   (Pearl   (Foxtail   (Sorghum)
                                 Millet)   Millet)

Subfamily: Chenopodioideae Amaranthoideae
Tribe: Atripliceae   Amarantheae
Genus: *Chenopodium*   *Amaranthus*

species: *durum*   *spelta*   *quinoa*   *caudatus*
(Name): (Durum   (Spelt)   (Quinoa)   (Amaranth)
              Wheat)   ✡
              ✡

15

The Origins of the Five Species

With the Family Tree Chart in mind, let's examine the grains both scientifically and *Halachically*.

Scientifically speaking, all of the *Chameshet Minei Dagan* are all in the family *Poaceae* of grasses. All of the cereal grains are in the subfamily of *Pooideae*. Spelt is considered a type of wheat, and it is in the same genus, *Triticum*. Barley and rye are quite closely related to them as well. All four are slightly down the family line in the *Triticeae* tribe. All four can cross-breed. Slightly less close in relation are oats, which as we saw have a far different appearance than the other grains. Even though oats will not crossbreed with the other four grains, they are still "all in the family", (or rather subfamily) of "Pooideae".

The Five Species all originated in the "Fertile Crescent", in which Israel just happens to be located. As for other grains, corn is actually part of the *Pooideae* subfamily too, but it originated in North America. It's the only other grain sharing that subfamily. Also in the family *Poaceae* are the rices, millets, and sorghum, none of which are indigenous to the Fertile Crescent. Teff and sorghum (a close millet relative) originated in Africa, wild rice (not a true "rice") in North America, and obviously Asian rice in Asia. Millets are from Asia and Africa. Lastly, the "Pseudocereals" are not

16

related, although they are considered grains. From Asia is "kasha" or buckwheat (not a true wheat), and from South America are amaranth and quinoa, (a type of amaranth).

Halacha holds the *Chameshet Minei Dagan* as being the only ones that apply to certain Jewish laws. Scientifically, the Five Grains indeed are all indigenous to Israel and no other types of grains are. Therefore, they still live up to their name of being the Five Grains of Israel, which is perfectly in line with Torah, to my happy surprise.

There are many species of all of the grains, (too many to list) but still all wheats are still wheat, all barleys are barley, etc. Note that "triticale" is a rye/wheat hybrid, (forbidden for Jews to create) and indigenous to *no place*. However, due to its familial origins, it is still subject to all the laws of the Five Grains, including *yashan*.

৪০৫৪০৫

Different Grains, Different Opinions?

But wait a minute! *Halachically* speaking, there seems to be a dispute among the *Rishonim* [early rabbis] as to which species are what grain types. In the *Gemara* (*Menachot* 70b), it says there are two types of wheat and three types of barley. Spelt is quoted as being a wheat, which is completely in line. After that, there are some problems...

The *Mishna* (*Pesachim* 35a), also mentions the Five Species. In the *Gemara* (ibid.), spelt is also correctly called a type of wheat. Rye is said to be a type of barley. This is fairly logical if you look at the plants. Then there's "shibbolet shu'al", which is generally translated as "oats". It is said to be a sub-species of *barley*!

The first problem is that our modern-day oats look nothing like a barley plant. (See the comparison of pictures on page 13.) Secondly, it was also translated, and called by a descriptive common name of "fox tails". If one looks at the oat plant at any stage, it has no resemblance to any part of a fox. Rabbi Gershom and Rashi in *Menachot* 70b, describe oats as they are today. The Rambam describes *shibbolet shu'al* as being a "2-rowed" type of barley, which

2-Row Barley (left) and 6-Row Barley (right). Some claim that 2-Row Barley could be the "oat" species of *Talmudic* times.

certainly isn't descriptive of today's oat plants. There is in fact, an actual species of barley called "2-Row Barley", (see picture on the opposite page). What a lot of confusion! Will the real oat plant please stand up? I found it very hard to believe, but science seems to be proving the identity of the Five Grains even better than the *Halachic* sources!

Whether *shibbolet shu'al* really means oats or not is perhaps to be debated, and actually has been by a few rabbis. Nonetheless, rabbinically speaking, oats in their present-day form, remain undeniably a *Halachically*-accepted species of the Five Grains. A good comparison of principle is this: Just as there is no actual *mesorah* [tradition] for the American turkey, it has all signs of being a kosher bird. The majority holds that turkey is indeed kosher and acceptable *Halachically*. So too with oats.

In any case, wheat, barley, spelt, rye and oats (or crosses between them) are the only grains that apply to the laws of *yashan*.

ဆဩဆဩ

The Yashan Cycle

Inevitably, the laws for *yashan* are dependent entirely on the Hebrew calendar. Interestingly, it is said that Hashem first thought of creation on the 1st of Nissan, and as everyone knows, He started physical Creation on the 1st of Tishrei. (*Gemara, Rosh Hashana* 10b-11a).

In Judaism, there is a civil or "fiscal new year", starting with *Rosh Hashana*, meaning the head or start of the year. That day, the 1st of Tishrei, is when the year number changes. Legal document dating, specific tithes, the seven-year *Sh'mittah* [Sabbatical year] cycles, and tenured land reverting back to its original owners are all calculated from this date. Just as all of these things are very physical in nature, the 1st of Tishrei is called, "the birthday of the world", when physical "life as we know it" was created.

The other new year on the 1st of Nissan, is considered a "spiritual new year". Similarly, *Rosh Chodesh* or the "head of the month", was the very first *mitzvah* given to the Jewish people, and instituted our Hebrew calendar. It's tied to the calculations of religious holidays, and ultimately the birth of the nation of Israel. When *Pesach* occurs, it is in the "month of spring", a time of redemption, when the birth of animals and sprouting of plants is at its peak. At the start of *Pesach*, its second day marks the milestones of the "Yashan Cycle".

Rabbis such as Rav Eliyahu Eliezer Dessler and Rabbi Moshe Chaim Luzzatto (the Ramchal) among many others, stated that time occurs in a spiral rather than being linear. Past and future meet at the present, all combining to create a spiritual connection, always spiraling upwards from Creation.

"Spiral Time" helps us visualize the "Cycle of Yashan".

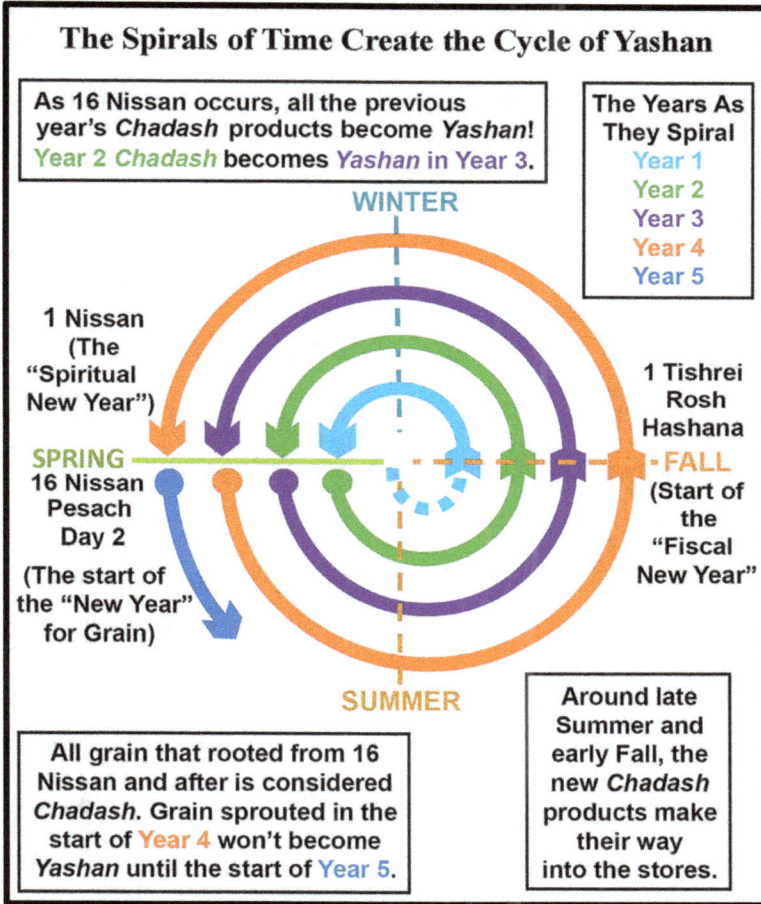

The Spirals of Time Create the Cycle of Yashan

As 16 Nissan occurs, all the previous year's *Chadash* products become *Yashan*! Year 2 *Chadash* becomes *Yashan* in Year 3.

The Years As They Spiral
Year 1
Year 2
Year 3
Year 4
Year 5

WINTER

1 Nissan (The "Spiritual New Year")

1 Tishrei Rosh Hashana

SPRING
16 Nissan Pesach Day 2

(The start of the "New Year" for Grain)

FALL (Start of the "Fiscal New Year"

SUMMER

All grain that rooted from 16 Nissan and after is considered *Chadash*. Grain sprouted in the start of Year 4 won't become *Yashan* until the start of Year 5.

Around late Summer and early Fall, the new *Chadash* products make their way into the stores.

Yashan = Seeds rooted before the 16 Nissan.

Chadash = Seeds rooted after 16 Nissan.

No grains can be eaten the year in which they sprouted until the next year. In the chart above, circles (16th of Nissan) show the start of a new year for grain. Arrows (ending just before in Spring) represent the end of a grain's year. As does life, the cycle always keeps on going.

Agricultural Laws Pertaining to Plants

Back in Biblical times, we lived in an agrarian society, and our livelihood and sustenance depended on it. One could easily realize Hashem was in control and not take eating or food for granted. There are many laws pertaining to farming, and all agree that the Torah's agricultural laws are still in full force for Israel to this day. Numerous sources in the *Talmud* relate how bread, *challah*, *chametz* and *matzah* are made from the Five Grains, defining them further as the sages write about them. Following are laws that pertain to plants. Most are the Seven Species, and especially the *Chameshet Minei Dagan*. Some have entire tractates dedicated to them in the *Talmud*, and their sources are too numerous to mention. (Agricultural laws on livestock have nothing to do with vintage grain, and are beyond the scope of this book.) Here are some basic laws on produce, listed in the order of where they first appear in the Torah.

✡ ***Making Matzah* and *Defining Chametz***: For 7 days you shall eat *matzah* [unleavened bread]/nullify and remove any *chametz* [leavening]. (*Shemot* [Numbers] 12:15, 13:3)

✡ ***The Mincha [Grain] Offerings***: When someone offers a Meal Offering (of wheat). (*Vayikra* 2:1-10)

✡ ***The Omer Barley Offering***: When you enter the Land and reap its harvest, you must bring an *Omer* of your first grain (barley), of ripe ears, toasted and ground, to offer a meal offering of first grain. (*Vayikra* 2:14-16, 23:9-14)

✿ ***Kalayim* [Prohibition of Mixing Species]**: This is where the sages determined grain sub-species due to an ability to cross-breed. The prohibition to create hybrids applies to all plants and animals. (*Vayikra* 19:19, *Devarim* 22:9)

✿ **The *Mitzvah* of *Yashan* [AKA "Prohibition of *Chadash*"]**: One can't eat bread or toasted grains until the day the Omer Offering is brought (on *Pesach* Day 2). It's an Eternal Decree in all dwelling places. (*Vayikra* 23:14)

✿ ***The First Fruits Offering of Shavuot***: On the 50th day after the *Omer* you must offer a meal offering (from the new crop of wheat). (*Vayikra* 23:16, *Bamidbar* 28:26)

✿ ***Taking Challah***: You must set aside a portion of dough made from the Five Grains. (*Bamidbar* 15:17-21)

✿ ***Terumah and Ma'aser, First Fruits***: All are tithes. (*Vayikra* 22:10-16, *Bamidbar* 5:9, *Devarim* 26:1-12).

✿ ***Arlah* [Forbidden Fruit]**: Fruit of trees after the first three years from planting can't be eaten. (Extends to fourth year fruits to be eaten in Jerusalem.) Applies to all fruits growing anywhere. (*Vayikra* 19:23-25)

✿ ***The Sh'mittah* [Sabbatical] *Year***: The Land must rest a year in every seven years. (*Vayikra* 25:1-7, 25:11-12).

✿ ***The Bracha* [Blessing] *of Birkat HaMazon***: When you eat and are satisfied, you must bless Hashem. (The *brachot* [blessings] of *HaMotzi, Borei Minei Mezonot,* and *Me'ein Shalosh* are rabbinic.) *Birkat HaMazon* is based on Israel's "praised" produce. (*Devarim* 8:10)

✿ ***Bal Tashchit* [Don't Destroy]**: Prohibition of destroying any type of fruit tree, this applies everywhere. It extends to destroying any useful item. (*Devarim* 20:19-20)

✿ ***Hungry Field Workers May Pluck By Hand***: They can't take any of the harvest home. (*Devarim* 23:25-26).

✿ ***Leave Some Harvest for the Poor***: (*Devarim* 24:19-22).

༺༒༺༒

Why Should Someone Keep Yashan?

You will be much more inclusive, and can host visiting rabbis and speakers that travel from Israel or big cities who keep *yashan.*

A *rebbetzin* [rabbi's wife] who didn't keep *yashan* once admitted to me, "You know Chasya, we really should keep *yashan*, it's in the Torah. *Chalav Yisrael* [dairy watched by a Jew] is only rabbinic."

In the past, when bread was a staple of life and *yashan* grain was hard to obtain, leniencies came about to keep Jews alive. The Torah always chooses life over death, therefore, many rabbis derived leniencies. In our times, *yashan* products are easier to obtain, however some people still consider it their *minhag* [custom] to refrain from keeping *yashan.* There are varying opinions we'll cover later. If one is unsure if they should, they can do it "b'li neder" [without a vow].

On a side note, one's pets and their food don't have to be *yashan.* Just as for kosher food, only Jewish humans must eat it.

Chapter 2

Foods for Thought

Typical Uses of the Grains: This is helpful to learn so that you know what products need to be checked to find out if they're *yashan*. Spelt and rye are winter crops in North America. They can often be in bread or crackers, although they're rarely used alone. One must make sure that there are no other added grains like *chadash* spring wheat. If grown in the USA or Canada, rye and spelt are almost always *yashan*.

Wheat: Winter wheat is often used to make hard items like crackers or hard pretzels. Spring wheat can be used to make fluffy items like bread or cake. Spring durum wheat is used mainly for pasta. Wheat gluten is used to make fake meat.

Oats: Often a spring crop, oats are the first of the grains to become *chadash* in the USA. Aside from cookies or cereal, oats can be in vegan items, and are often an ingredient in "gluten-free" foods.

Barley: Barley can be a winter crop or a spring crop. It can sometimes be found in flavored tea bags or soy drinks.

Malt: Barley malt or "malt" is sprouted, dried, aged and roasted. In large amounts, it's used in beer (from 2-Row Barley). In small amounts, it's added to flour for its chemical properties, such as to facilitate rising. In this case, it may be *batul* [nullified] since it's a tiny amount– 1% or less. Malt is sweet and dark, and can be used as flavoring or coloring. For these purposes, there may be too much to be *batul*.

Later, we talk about *minhagim* [customs] and varying customs for malt. Some are strict and say malt is never *batul*. A few say it's always *batul*. (*Minhagim* starts on page 36.)

After harvest, the winnowed whole grains in their husks, referred to as "hulled" grain, (below) are ready to process.

| Rye | Spelt | Oats | Wheat | Barley |

Are There Foods That Are Always Yashan?

Fortunately, there are! Most matzah, matzah meal, and gefilte fish made from matzah meal, are usually *yashan*. (See page 32.) Aged whiskey is always *yashan*, as it has gone through at least one *Pesach*. Most regular vinegar in the USA is made from corn and should be *yashan*, but check the ingredient labels for sure.

All purely winter wheat is *yashan*. One must make sure that flour is indeed made with purely winter wheat, even if it says so on the label. Many Jewish companies store flour to ensure it is *yashan*. Some mainstream flours can be *yashan*, depending on mill location. Regardless, all products should be checked to ensure their status hasn't changed. Draught, infestation or diseases occur that affect crops. For example, recently some companies that make normally-*yashan* flours have been adding spring wheat to improve their product due to low-quality crops. Despite the ingredients saying "pure winter wheat", that's not always the case. According to federal regulations, companies can legally add *chadash* spring wheat to increase protein quality, even up to 50%, and can still say "pure winter wheat"! Just like fruit juices that say 100% juice, there can be other things mixed in. So too with 100% winter wheat. This is why flour without *yashan hashgacha* [kosher supervision for *yashan*] needs to be checked in the *Guide to Chodosh*, a publication that reports if products are *yashan* or how to tell if they are by date codes.

Products not containing any of the Five Grains are considered to be just like they're *yashan*. Unfortunately, some grain ingredients aren't obvious by their "scientific-sounding" names. One should look over the "Grain Derivatives List" on page 31. It can be surprising to learn there's wheat in your potato chips, barley in tea, and oats in your gluten-free veggie burger.

ᏰᎧᏳᏰᎧᏳ

Why Gluten-Free Can Still Be Chadash

"Gluten-free" seems to be the catch phrase these days. Although, just because a food does not contain gluten, that doesn't mean they are "Five Grain-free". There is still a possibility that they could be *chadash*. Oats are found in many "gluten-free" products. (The oat controversies continue…) Oats have notably less gluten, or are sometimes gluten-free. However, they are the first of the crops to become a *chadash* problem in the USA. I have seen several different sources, and there seems to be some disagreement as to whether oats are naturally gluten-free or not. (Of the sources that say that they are gluten-free, they also claim that oats aren't native to the Fertile Crescent.) Some say oats are gluten-free, but have been cross-contaminated with other gluten-containing grains. Others claim oats have gluten, but very little. (Note that nearly anything "multigrain" usually contains oats.)

Another gluten-free item is wheat grass used for juicing and in vitamins. It is certainly one of the Five Grains. (More on pages 40-42.) The moral of this story? Always read the ingredient label!

ဆၢငᏮဆၢငᏮ

Potentially Chadash Items

The following items in the table below can always be a problem. All their date codes must be checked in the *Guide*:

Potential Chadash Products and Their Grains			
Spring Wheat	**Oats**	**Barley**	**Barley Malt**
Bread, Bagels and Tortillas	Gluten-Free Products	Flavored Tea in Bags	Bread and Bagels
Pasta/Noodles	Multigrain Items	Soy Milk	Vegan Drinks
Whole Wheat Flour	Rolled, Quick or Instant Oats	Whole-Grain Breads	Doughnuts and Cookies
Spicy Fries	Baby Food in Jars	Soups	Tea
Durum, Kamut or Khorasan Wheat	Crackers and Cookies	Multi-Grain Cereals	White or All-Purpose Flour
Pastry Dough or Pastry Flour	Vegetarian Products	Brown Rice Syrup	Corn or Rice Cereals
Rye Bread or Rye Crackers	Health and Energy Bars	Brewer's Yeast	Beer, Ale, Malt Beverages
Any Cereals	Any Cereals	Any Cereals	Malt Vinegar

Reference List of Possible Chadash Products

Check ingredients on these potentially problem items. If they contain any of the Five Grains, look it up in the *Guide*.

Alcoholic Beverages; Artisan Breads; Breaded Foods; Brown Rice Syrup; Candy; Chocolates; Condiments; Corn Bread; Corn Flake Cereals; Corn Flake Crumbs; Dry Powdered Mustard; Dry-Roasted Nuts & Seeds; Flour; French Fries; Gluten-Free Products; Gravy & Gravy Mixes; Kosher Vitamin Supplements; Ice Creams; Imitation Crab; Licorice; Liquors; Malt Vinegar; Multi-Grain Cereals; Multi-Grain "Corn" Tortilla Chips; Multi-Grain Tortillas; Oat Milk; Potato Chips; Prepared Soups (canned or frozen); Processed Lunch Meats; Pudding & Pie Fillings; Puffed Rice Cereals; Rotisserie Seasoning Blends; Rye Bread; Rye Crackers; Salad Dressings; Sauces; Sausages; Seasoned Chips & Snacks; Soup/Dip Mixes; Soup Cubes; Soy Sauce (contained wheat may be *batul*); Spice Blends; Spicy Fries; Vegan Meat Substitutes; Vitamins.

ಬಂಧಬಂಧ

Possible Chadash Products from Foreign Crops

All wheat, barley and oat products still apply. If imported to the USA from other countries (except Israel and Canada), these may be *chadash*. Rye Bagels; Rye Bagel Chips; Rye Bread; Rye Buns; Rye Crackers; Rye Bread Dough; Rye Pretzels, Spelt Cereal; Spelt Bread; Spelt Crackers; Spelt Flour; Spelt Matzah.

Reference List of Problematic Ingredients

These can potentially be *chadash*. If any of them appear in a product's ingredient list, check for allergen information. If it's made from one of the Five Grains check the date codes.

All-Purpose Flour; Ancient Grains; Barley; Barley Flour; Barley Grass; Barley Malt; Bleached Flour; Bran; Bran Flour; Bread Crumbs; Bread Flour; Brewer's Yeast; Bromated Flour; Brown Flour; Bulgur; Bulgur Wheat; Cake Flour; Cake Meal; Couscous; Cracked Wheat; Cracker Meal; Dextrin; Durum; Durum Flour; Durum Wheat; Einkorn; Emmer; Enriched Flour; Farina; Farro; Flour; Food Starch; Glucose Syrup; Gluten; Gluten Flour; Graham; Graham Cracker; Graham Flour; Hydrolyzed Wheat Protein; Kamut; Kamut Flour; Kamut Wheat; Khorasan Wheat; Khorasan Flour; Malt; Malted Barley; Malt Flavoring; Maltodextrin; Malt Vinegar; Modified Food Starch; Oat Bran; Oat Flour; Oat Grass; Oat Grass Juice; Oatmeal; Oats; Orzo; Pearled Barley; Pearled Wheat; Phosphated Flour; Rolled Oats; Rye; Rye Bran; Rye Flour; Seitan; Self-Rising Flour; Semolina; Spelt; Spelt Bran; Spelt Flour; Spelt Germ; Spelt Grass; Sprouted Grain; Starch; Steel-Cut Oats; Tabouleh; Triticale; Triticum; Unbleached Flour; Vegetable Protein; Vegetable Starch; Vital Gluten; Wheat; Wheat Berries; Wheat Bran; Wheat Flour; Wheat Germ; Wheat Gluten, Wheat Grass; Wheat Grass Juice; Wheat Grass Powder; Wheat Starch; White Flour; Whole Grains; Whole Wheat; Whole Wheat Flour.

Grain Derivatives Reference List

These items can depend on what they are made of. Some may have scientific-sounding names. Sometimes they are made from the Five Grains, sometimes they are made out of other items like corn or rice. One key to deciphering this is to look at the "food allergens" under the ingredients. If it lists "wheat", it has a wheat derivative. Imported items containing these must be checked on to see if they are *yashan* or not. When marked as such, certain derivatives do not pose a problem if made in the USA or in Israel with reliable *hashgacha*. These items may not even be a problem, but they should be checked just to be sure. (They could be *batul*, so ask your rabbi).

Ingredients Possibly Derived from Wheat: Dextrin; Food Starch; Glucose Syrup (more often from Europe); HVP or Hydrolyzed Vegetable Protein; Inulin (dietary fiber source); Maltodextrin (rarely in the USA); Modified Food Starch; Starch; TVP or Textured Vegetable Protein (rarely in the USA); Xanthan Gum (can be fed with wheat bacteria); Yeast Extract (common in Europe, but rarely if ever in the USA).

Ingredients Possibly Derived from Barley: Beta Glucan (dietary fiber source); Brewer's Yeast; Brown Rice Syrup; Yeast Extract made from Brewer's Yeast (rarely in the USA).

Ingredients Possibly Derived from Oats: Beta Glucan (dietary fiber source).

Yashan Ingredients

Yes, there is good news, none of the following pose a problem and are all considered *yashan.*

Amaranth; Autolyzed Yeast; Baker's Yeast; Buckwheat or "Kasha"; Corn; Millet; Quinoa; Rice; Teff; Torula Yeast; Wild Rice.

ဆာ‌ကြဆာကြ

Products That Are Always Yashan

✡ Purely winter wheat, rye or spelt from the USA and Canada. (Check the *Guide* for status of winter wheat products, and look at the ingredient panel to be sure nothing else is added along with the rye and spelt).

✡ All products made in Israel with a trusted and reliable *hechsher* [kosher symbol].

✡ Products marked "Yoshon" or "Kemach Yashan" (in Hebrew or English) with reliable kosher certification.

✡ Most gefilte fish; most matzah and matzah meal (except "Kerry" brand, which is not made of real matzah).

✡ Meal Mart brand hospital or airline meals and frozen products.

✡ All Kemach brand flours. This even includes the malt.

Note: Flours and other products that don't have *yashan hashgacha* need to be checked out in the *Guide* for date codes. Although they may be listed as using pure winter wheat, crop situations can arise to effect protein content. Some companies add *chadash* spring wheat to compensate.

Average Timing

Although all grains that took root after the second day of *Pesach* are *chadash*, one can roughly estimate a product's status. Freshly baked items can be affected by location.

The timing is different every single year, so there is no set rule as to the actual dates at which items become *yashan*. This is more related to the Hebrew calendar than the weather and crop conditions. Since the calendar fluctuates from year to year, the secular date always changes for the second day of *Pesach*. Therefore, there is never any actual fixed date for when an item will become *chadash*. Yet another reason to check out the date codes in the *Guide*. Once one has been keeping *yashan* for a few seasons, they get to know the local food trends. It's still a good idea to prepare well in advance.

In the *Guide*, the "chadash date" or cut-off date is just that– the date at which an item *becomes chadash*. This means that an item with a date of the day before or earlier than the given date is *yashan*. On the given date and afterwards it will be *chadash*. The chart below gives an idea of a general time frame of *chadash* cut-off dates. This is only a sample. A current *Guide* must always be consulted.

General Cut-Off Dates Chart for Various Items	
(This sample is NOT to be used to determine current Yashan Status)	
Product	**Chadash Cut-Off Date**
Oat Products (Oats ONLY without other grains)	
Oats, Oatmeal, Cookies, Most Cereals, etc.	**July 22**
Wheat Products (Wheat products ONLY without other grains)	
Flour, Spring Wheat and Wheat Gluten	**August 1**
Pasta & Noodles	**August 15**
Wheat Germ	**August 1**
Wheat Starch	**Yashan**
Wheat Starch (*L'Chumra*) [for those who want to be strict]	**August 15**
Winter Wheat Products ONLY (No other added grains)	**Yashan**
Matzah	**Yashan**
Matzah Meal	**Yashan**
Gefilte Fish	**Yashan**
Barley Products (Barley ONLY without other grains)	
Barley and products containing Barley Cereals containing Barley	**August 9**
Barley Malt Products (Barley Malt ONLY without other grains)	
Products containing Malt, Barley Malt, or Barley Malt Extract	**December 15**
Beer (Does not apply to Wheat beer.)	**November 15**

It should be noted that freshly baked wheat items go by a "purchase date". This also varies, but is often around August 1st for the Eastern USA, and August 12th in the West.

Items That Are Never Yashan

Spring wheat and spring barley crops will always be a potential *chadash* problem, no matter where they are grown. This is why it's so important to check the dates on items made from any kind of wheat or barley. Since oats are often planted in spring as well, they have a potential to be *chadash*, more so in fact, being the first crop to be harvested in the USA.

There are some potentially problem ingredients (such as wheat grass shown below), that can depend entirely on a person's *minhag*. We will cover them in detail in a few pages.

What does one do with a product that is not *yashan*? One way around it is to purchase it before *Pesach* and store it until afterward. It would then have to be sold for *Pesach*. Very perishable items like bread should be wrapped extremely well (even multiple times) and preferably kept in a sub-zero or manual-defrost freezer to keep fresh.

Wheat grass in a pot (left) grown for juice (right). This ingredient could be a potential *chadash* problem. (For details, see page 40.)

Ingredients Affected by Minhag

There are some ingredients that depend entirely on a person's custom as to their *yashan* or *chadash* status. We will examine all the different rabbinic views. I am not a rabbi, and I cannot give a *p'sak* [*Halachic* ruling], nor do I recommend any specific opinion. Each person must ask their own individual rabbi or favored *kashrut* agency. I am simply presenting the various views, with the reasons behind each one so that they all can be easily understood.

Wheat Starch: (Not to be confused with "wheat germ".) This is often used as a thickening agent, but can also be used as an emulsifier. It can be used as a filler or even a binder in some processed meats. This is a very common ingredient in all kinds of processed foods. It was originally believed to be made from spring wheat and that it could be *chadash*. It has recently been discovered that this is likely not the case. There are two different views. Ask your Rav how he holds.

Wheat Starch is Always Yashan: This is a more lenient view. According to the *Guide*, wheat starch might not be made from spring wheat, based on the following:

1. There's no advantage to use spring wheat instead of winter wheat.

2. Spring wheat is far more valuable for using as flour for fluffy bread products and the like.

3. Winter wheat is the majority crop. About 70% of the USA wheat crop is winter wheat. Availability and lower cost increases its likelihood to be used for wheat starch.

The *Guide* goes by the *safek safeika* [double doubt] of the Rema, in assuming that the wheat starch could have been from last year, or if freshly milled it is most likely from *yashan* winter wheat. Several rabbis were consulted on this. (A "double doubt" is always permitted.)

Wheat Starch Could be Chadash: This is a more stringent view, called "l'chumra" [to be stringent]. Since it is not a complete certainty that the wheat starch is *yashan*, some people still prefer to be strict. They treat wheat starch like spring wheat, as having the same general *chadash* cut-off date for spring wheat. For those with this view, all date codes must be checked when wheat starch is an ingredient.

Wheat starch is an ingredient found in many products, having a variety of uses.

Barley Malt: This ingredient has several different names—malt, barley malt, malted barley, barley malt extract, malt extract. Usually, anything with the word "malt" refers to barley malt, although other grains such as wheat and rye can be malted too. (Products using other grains will generally state what kind of grain has been malted.)

"Malting" is the process of sprouting barley grains. Since this process takes some time, the *chadash* dates for malt are a lot later than for barley itself. The process of "malting" takes up to 3-months. First, it is dried slightly to increase germination, then sprouted and dried again. It can also be roasted. This gives it a dark color which enables it to be used for coloring. It has a unique, sweet taste, and is used for flavoring foods like corn flakes. In larger quantities, it is used for specialty vinegars and beer. Beer is usually made with 2-Row Barley instead of 6-Row Barley.

The *minhag* concerning malt is not so much based on the ingredient itself as it is the *amount* of the ingredient. Malt can be added to flour for its chemical properties, facilitating the rising action in bread and cakes. However, it is a very tiny amount- sometimes only 1% or less of the makeup of the flour. On the other hand, when malt is used as flavoring or coloring, the amount may be too great to be *batul*.

There are at least three different opinions on this. Always ask your Rav how to hold.

Malt is Always Batul: Some say that malt used as an additive, coloring or minor flavoring, is always *batul*, due to the small amount. This does not apply to products using larger amounts of malt, like beer and malt vinegar.

Malted Barley Can be Batul, but Not Always: An intermediate view, there are those that say if malt is used as a chemical agent only, (as with flour), it is *batul*. However, if malt is used as a coloring agent or a flavoring, there is too large of an amount that is added and is not *batul*. In this latter case, the date codes must be checked.

Malted Barley is Never Batul: Some are strict and say that malt is never *batul*. One who holds this view, must check the date codes on the product any time malt is an ingredient.

Barley during the malting process.

Sprouted Grain and Grain Grasses: Relatively new to the health foods scene, "sprouted grain" is said to have more nutritional value than normally processed grain and is easier to digest. It can be made with one or all of the Five Grains.

Another new "superfood" is grain grass. All five grains are used, but wheat is the most common. Grain seeds are put in a planter of dirt and left to grow. Only the leaves are used, not the seed or root, (except barley). The main use is for juicing and smoothies, but can be an ingredient in vitamins. It's grown as-is, or sold as powder and frozen juice. There are vastly different opinions as to whether grain grasses are a *yashan* problem or not.

"Sprouted grain" is a bit different. To make it, grain seeds are soaked in water until they have a tiny white root just starting to sprout, which is the time the germinating seed has its highest nutrient content. It's at this point when these sprouting grains are processed, locking in the extra nutrients. It can take a little over two days from sprouting to final processing, so the timing is very short.

There are two different methods used for the processing:

1. For the "dry method", grains are sprouted as mentioned above, then dried, and lastly, they are ground into flour.

2. For the "wet" method to produce items like bread, the fresh sprouts are ground into a pasty dough and added to other ingredients like soy flour to make the finished product.

I've researched these issues thoroughly, contacting multiple rabbis. According to most opinions for both sprouted grain and grasses, *Halachically*, there is no problem if a grain seed was already *yashan*. Let's see the opinions and conditions...

The majority opinion on both of these issues is as follows: A grain seed that was already *yashan* does not become *chadash* simply due to its sprouting. That particular grain seed remains permissible. However, if it took root after the second day of *Pesach* (or two weeks prior according to other opinions) and grew into a plant, only *that plant's* resulting grain seeds would be *chadash*. There are other views however. Always ask a Rav how to hold!

Sprouted Grains and Grass Are Yashan: The condition for this is that one must be certain the grain seed used is already *yashan*. This way, if the seed sprouts, even though it's after the 16th of Nissan, the seed itself still remains *yashan*. The sprouting action is irrelevant to the status of the final product, presuming that all other ingredients were *yashan*. Some with this view hold grains can't be sprouted in soil, only in water.

For grasses, most rabbis hold that there is no problem at all with the leaves. Some even hold that the grain used for the grass doesn't even need to be *yashan* beforehand.

Sprouted Grains Are Like Other Grains: A less common view goes by the date of production of the final product like normal grains. Some hold that since they sprout in water, they're not in the same category. Just as hydroponic vegetables don't have a *bracha* [blessing] of *Pri HaAdamah* [fruit of the ground], this opinion says that due to never having been in soil, the prohibition of *chadash* doesn't apply, at least in the Diaspora. The general *chadash* cut-off dates in the *Guide* are followed for the grain type used. For multiple grains, the earliest date applies.

Sprouted Grain and Grass May Be Chadash: This view holds that there is a doubt, and sprouted grain may be *chadash* since they could have sprouted after second day *Pesach*. The only way to be sure about a sprouted grain product's status is to call the *kashrut* agency that does the *hashgacha* on it.

For grain grasses, many say that even though only the leaves are used, they are still the Five Grains and fall under the prohibition of *chadash*. This view allows it only if the seeds are already *yashan*. The strictest opinion says that the issue is compounded if it is a Jew growing the grass for home use, it makes it a Jewish grain crop.

If one wants to be safe, it never hurts to go the strictest route possible. Perhaps the best idea for those wanting to grow their own grain grass, is to plant the seeds two weeks before *Pesach*. Sell it all over the holiday, and after *Pesach* it will be *yashan*. Ask your Rav!

Sprouted grains: *Yashan* or *chadash*?

Chapter 3

Is It Realistic?

Is Keeping Yashan Right for You? Before actually committing to keeping *yashan*, you may want to ask yourself some questions. Below is a handy questionnaire:

1. *Do you feel that keeping yashan is the right thing to do?*

2. *Do you have the means to buy extra food to stock up?*

3. *Are you able to pay a bit more for yashan products?*

4. *Do you have adequate space to keep foods fresh while they are in storage?*

5. *Are you able to cook at home more often or are willing to give up certain foods if you run out?*

6. *Can you forego having dinner with someone if they don't want to go to a yashan-certified restaurant? If not, are you comfortable with suggesting a different place or ordering something that wouldn't be a yashan issue?*

7. *Are you willing to ask hosts, caterers or waiters if certain foods or ingredients are yashan, and to tell people that you have dietary restrictions?*

8. *If you are married, are you okay with your spouse not keeping yashan if they don't want to, even if you do?*

9. Are you confident you can keep yashan if you travel?

10. Do you live in Israel or plan to move there?

There is no right or wrong answer to any of these questions, but they may help you figure out if keeping *yashan* is the best thing for you. (With the exception of the last question, you still have a choice.) Most people face these situations at some point, so you should be prepared to deal with them. If you feel comfortable with this, then you should really have no problem. The next few sections may just help you decide if keeping *yashan* is right for you.

৪০৫৪৩০৫৪

Factors That Affect Keeping the *Mitzvah*

All of the questions above and the sections below play a part in keeping *yashan*. If you aren't up to it, you should perhaps think twice, because it is life-changing. If you just want to try it out to see if you can do it, then at first take it on *b'li neder*. That is a good thing to do regardless.

৪০৫৪৩০৫৪

Where You Live Determines How You Keep It

It sounds quite odd, but where you're living really does affect how you will keep this *mitzvah*. Below we will look at how different places are conducive for certain things.

Let's review the variables...

The Diaspora vs. Israel

If you live in Israel and keep kosher, you are in all likelihood keeping *yashan*. In Israel, it is a breeze to keep *yashan*, which is good. It is a mandatory *mitzvah* there due to being one of the Torah's agricultural laws, as was covered in the first chapter. Since all the laws of crops have to be kept in Israel, all the major, reliable Israeli *kashrut* agencies make sure that everything is indeed *yashan*.

The only problem with food in Israel is imported products. Since Israelis don't have to worry about keeping *yashan*, less knowledgeable people ordering items from abroad may not even be aware of the *mitzvah* in order to deal with it properly. This means that if they import goods from other countries including the USA, what is shipped could be *chadash*. Therefore, one must pay extra attention to imported products. Check the *Guide* for specific products, or look at "*Yashan in Various Countries*" in the last chapter (starting on page 134), to help determine if an imported product may be *yashan*. Any imported item must follow the same date codes as its country of origin.

If you live in Israel and visit *chutz L'Aretz* [outside the Land], you must keep *yashan* wherever you are visiting. It's a good idea to contact someone ahead of time to make sure there are *yashan* products available.

If you live in the Diaspora and visit Israel, you still have to keep *yashan* while you are in *Eretz Yisrael*.

Large Cities vs. Small Jewish Pockets

If you live in a large city, especially with a big Jewish population, it is the next best thing to living in Israel. There will most likely be Jewish brands available that have *hashgacha* specifically for *yashan*. There may even be *yashan* bakeries and restaurants. A local *kashrut* agency will usually have a list of establishments that cater to *yashan* consumers.

As for small pockets of Jewish communities, it can sometimes be a challenge. The main thing is to be able to have access to what you need. Hopefully there will be at least some kind of a kosher section in a grocery store. Even many Walmart stores have one in their "Ethnic Foods" aisle. Some people travel to the nearest city with a fairly large Jewish population to buy Jewish brands of food and kosher meat. Some areas have a co-op that deals in kosher food with a higher standard such as *chalav Yisrael* dairy products, or "hard-to-get" items like *chalak Beit Yosef* meats [*Sefardi* standard of kosher meat] and *yashan* baked goods.

For those without a solid Jewish community, having a freezer is a good idea. Nowadays with the internet, there are online Jewish grocery stores that carry many kosher products. This may be a good alternative, and generally the more one buys, the cheaper it can be. For those that don't have kosher meat available, vegan food is also an option up to a certain point. Unfortunately, most "fake meat" is made from wheat gluten, so it is important to read the ingredient labels. For wheat or oat-containing products, check the date codes in the *Guide*. One must plan ahead and stock up. Specialty stores like Trader Joe's and larger health food stores sometimes carry kosher meat and vegan products, but one must be sure to check for a reliable *hechsher*. If vegan "meat" is unavailable, unflavored dry TVP (made from soy) is great. If it has no additives, it doesn't even need a *hechsher*, as it's considered like a flour, but has no problematic ingredients.

෨෬෨෬

Eastern USA vs. Western USA

Products become *chadash* earlier in the Eastern USA and later in the West. This is especially true for freshly baked items like bread and cookies. It is said that wheat flour in bakeries of the Western USA can contain *chadash* mixtures at any time. The general flow of products reaches the West later, with some still-*yashan* frozen products being found throughout the whole *chadash* season. It takes extra time to ship items to the west, so by the time they reach their destination, they are already often around two weeks older.

Flour from specific factories known for *yashan* winter wheat can to be found throughout the USA, so if one cooks their food the old-fashioned way- from scratch, one should easily be able to keep *yashan*.

Chumra vs. Commandment

One thing is for certain, anyone living in Israel or who visits there, *must keep yashan*! It's a commandment since it is an agricultural law. Elsewhere, for couples and families, it can be trickier. It is said that one cannot force a family member to take on a *chumra* [an extra, personal stringency that a person observes on their own initiative]. If spouses disagree on it, that may be an issue. What if one believes it is a *mitzvah* and the other thinks it's a *chumra*? In this case, they should probably take counsel with their rabbi. One really should anyway, because not only do some feel that keeping *yashan* (or not) is a *minhag*, but there are ingredients affecting *yashan* status that have to do with *minhagim* as well.

𝄢𝄢𝄢

Customs and Minhagim

Following are relevant views of many *rabbanim* [rabbis] about *yashan* in the Diaspora, although this is not an exhaustive list. Rabbis are listed in order of when they lived, and how they held.

---

[1] Note: Although Rav Ovadiah Yosef, z"l held one should keep *yashan* everywhere, he also held that if there was a doubt about something being *yashan* from outside of Israel, then it may be permissible even in Israel. *See Yalkut Yosef -* הלכות חדש, סימן רצג, אות יא׳

יא איסור אכילה מתבואה חדשה חל הן על תבואות של ארץ ישראל, והן על תבואות של חוץ לארץ, לכן ראוי ונכון לחקור על מיני תבואה המובאים מחוץ לארץ, המשווקים כיום בארץ, ואשר מיוצרים בחוץ לארץ מתבואות חוץ לארץ, וכגון קווקרים, גרנולה, דברי מאפה, בירה, וכדו׳, שבכל אלה יש בהם חשש לאיסור חדש, אולם כל זה לכתחלה, אבל בדיעבד כל ש״יש ספק אם יש בו איסור חדש, יש להקל גם לדידן. וידוע שבזמנינו אין מצוי חדש בארץ ישראל, שאין תבואה שנזרעת אחר הפסח ונקצרת קודם הפסח הבא.

[ואיסור חדש מצוי בעיקר בחו"ל, וכן בארץ ישראל מצוי איסור זה בקמח המיובא מחו"ל].

[ילקו"י הל׳ שעטנז סי׳ רצג]

Rabbis Who Held *Yashan* Does Not Apply in the Diaspora	Rabbis Who Held One Must Keep *Yashan* Everywhere
Rav Shalom Shachna	Rif (Yitzchak Alfasi)
Maharshal (Shlomo Luria)	Rambam/Maimonides (Moshe ben Maimon)
Rema (Moshe Isserles)	Rashba (Shlomo ben Aderet)
Maharal of Prague (Yehudah Loew)	Rosh (Asher ben Yehiel)
Bach (Yoel ben Shmuel Yaffe-Sirkis)	Tur/Ba'al HaTurim (Yacov ben Asher)
Taz (David HaLevi Segal)	Ran (Nissim ben Reuven of Girona)
Magen Avraham (Avraham Aveli Gombiner)	Beit Yosef/Shulchan Aruch (Yosef Karo)
The Aruch HaShulchan (Yechiel Michel Epstein)	Shach (Shabtai ben Meir HaKohen)
Lubavitcher Rebbe (Menachem Mendel Schneerson)	The P'nei Yehoshua (Yaakov Yehoshua Falk)
Rabbi Yosef Dov (Joseph Ber) Soloveitchik	Sha'agat Aryeh (Arye Leib ben Asher)
	Gra/Vilna Ga'on (Eliyahu ben Shlomo Zalman)
	Chida (Chaim Yosef David Azulai)
	Rabbi Akiva Eiger
	The Beit HaLevi (Yosef Dov Soloveitchik)
	Chazan Ish (Avraham Yeshaya Karelitz)
	Brisker Rav (Yitzchok Zev Soloveitchik)
	Rabbi Eliezer Silver
	Rav Yaakov Kamenetzsky
	Rav Aaron Soloveitchik
	Rav Ovadiah Yosef [1]

Typically, most *Sefardim* [Jews of Spanish, Middle Eastern, and African descent] have the *minhag* to keep *yashan*. Many *Ashkenazim* [Jews of European descent] and most *Chassidim* [Ultra-Orthodox Jews] don't. There's a growing trend among *Ashkenazi yeshivot* [religious school for boys and men] to keep *yashan*. One generally follows the customs of their rabbi.

৩০০৩৩০০৩

Rabbinic Opinions in Support of Keeping Yashan

Many rabbis who keep *yashan* feel that it's a Torah commandment; an "everlasting covenant in all your dwelling places" that applies in any location and at any time, and it is not merely just a *chumra*. Those of us who keep *yashan* generally agree with this. As seen in the chart, there are twice the number of rabbis in support of it. It's interesting to note that the Besht (Baal Shem Tov) initially held that one didn't need to keep *yashan* in the Diaspora, however he later retracted this opinion after he met Rabbi Yechiel of Horodna who kept it. (That must have been some conversation!) Another *Chassidic* giant, Rav Shneur Zalman of Liadi, was also strict to keep it. A *Chabad* rabbi once told me, "I don't know why we aren't strict with *yashan*, we're strict with everything else!"

Although not stating that keeping *yashan* in the Diaspora is preferable, Rav Moshe Feinstein and the Chafetz Chaim (Rabbi Israel Meir Kagan) said that one should ideally try to be strict. However, Rav Feinstein added that if only *chadash* is available, people shouldn't be told that they can't eat it.

The Maharam (Rabbi Meir ben Baruch) and Rav Yaakov Kamenetzsky viewed keeping *yashan* to be a *chumra*. However, they were strict about keeping it themselves! All of these great rabbis did not publicize their keeping *yashan*, and urged those who keep the *mitzvah* to do so discreetly. We'll look at more on this in Chapter 7 on page 129.

𝕤𝕠𝕔𝕤𝕤𝕠𝕔𝕤

Views Supporting Not Keeping Yashan

There are varying opinions as to whether the *Mitzvah* of *Yashan* applies only in *Eretz Yisrael* or only to Jewish-grown crops. The Bach held that the prohibition of *chadash* doesn't apply to non-Jewish crops at all, others say this is true especially if it's grown outside of Israel. The most widely accepted view is of the Rema, that *chadash* is a *sefek sefeika*, as it *could have* been planted early enough and *may* be permitted in *chutz L'Aretz*. The two factors make it a *sefek sefeika*, and a "double doubt" is always permitted.

Another opinion is if there are extenuating circumstances such as conflicting growing seasons, it is a hardship to obtain, or there's a scarcity of *yashan* grain, one can rely on the lenient view due to potential starvation. Others feel that since it was decided upon by certain rabbis to be lenient outside of Israel, it is a tradition to be continued.

What is "Yashan Hashgacha"?

This is a common question people ask when trying to look up the date codes from the *Guide*. A lot of people don't understand what it means when a product has "no yashan hashgacha". It confused some into thinking that perhaps the product wasn't even kosher, when this is not the case at all. Let's take a look at what *yashan hashgacha* really is.

When a company is "kosher-certified", it is said to have "hashgacha". More accurately, it has "kashrut hashgacha", meaning it is being supervised by a *mashgiach* [supervisor] for being kosher. In the case of *yashan hashgacha*, it's a bit more complex. The *mashgiach* is hired specifically to make sure that all ingredients are *yashan* as well as kosher.

A product can have *hashgacha* and be kosher but it still may not be *yashan*. If a certified product has *yashan hashgacha*, one doesn't have to worry about checking date codes. It's automatically *yashan*, or at least to some degree. Certain *kashrut* agencies have *yashan hashgacha*, although this is not all that common in the USA. Of those agencies that do, one can rely on products with their *hechsher* to be *yashan*. We'll look at some of these agencies shortly.

There are varying degrees of *yashan hashgacha*. One can tell which products fit into each category in the *Guide* by the designated Hebrew letter appearing in front of it...

✡ Some *hechsherim* [*kashrut* agency symbols] make sure that all products and their ingredients are *yashan*. (This is category "א" in the *Guide*.)

✡ Others only have *hashgacha* on certain products, and will mark "Yashan", "ישן", or "Yoshon" on the label. One agency may oversee many products, some *yashan* and others not. It is for this reason that one has to make sure "Yashan" is printed on the package as well as the agency's *hechsher*. (This is category "ב" in the *Guide*, meaning check the label for the word "Yashan".)

✡ Another category of *Yashan Hashgacha* has to do with *minhag*. Certain agencies make sure that all wheat, oats, barley, rye or spelt ingredients in a product are *yashan*, but consider any barley malt to be *batul* due to the small amount used. (See pages 38-39 in Chapter 2 about barley malt.) Therefore, they do not check on the status of malt. Usually one must also check for the word "Yashan", "ישן", or "Yoshon" on the label as well. (This is also category "ב" in the *Guide*. One who is strict about malt must check the date codes given in the *Guide*. One who is not, won't need to.)

✡ The last category is a product without any *yashan hashgacha*, so the date codes must be checked in the

Guide. It's kosher, but the *yashan* status of the ingredients hasn't been looked into at all. (This is category "ד" in the *Guide*– "No yashan hashgacha", which only pertains to *yashan* status, not kosher status.) This is the case with most mainstream brands and their products.

ଘଠଘଠ

Are There "Yashan-Only" Hechsherim?

There are agencies with *yashan hashgacha* in various categories. It's not an exhaustive list, but here are samples...

Reliable "Always-Yashan" Hechsherim from Israel: If you see these or any other reliable *hechsherim* on products *made in Israel*, it means they are automatically *yashan*.

Rabbi Moshe Landau
of B'nei Brak

Badatz Mehadrin

Bet Din Zedek
Bet Yosef

Chug Chatam Sofer
of B'nei Brak

"Always-Yashan" Hechsherim in Any Packing Location:
The following agencies thoroughly check every ingredient
for *yashan* status no matter where the item was packaged.

Eida Hachereidis Badatz of Yerushalayim

Rabbi E. L. Schneebalg of Edgeware, UK

Kedassia of London

Rabbi O. Y. Westheim of Manchester

The following two groupings of *hechsher* categories are
conditional, meaning that they are only *yashan* with specific
guidelines. They all must exhibit the word "ישן" in Hebrew
or "Yashan" in English (or often the *Ashkenazi* "Yoshon" in
English) on the label. (See the list on pages 53-54 for how
they're categorized in the *Guide* by Hebrew letter.) Some
agencies supervise hundreds of companies and products. Since
most are not *yashan*, the conditional criteria must be followed.

Hechsherim That Are Yashan-Only When "Yashan" Is Printed on the Label, Including Malt: These agencies oversee many products, some just for *kashrut*, others for *yashan* status, however they do check the status of malt. Since *hashgacha* is on both *yashan* and non-*yashan* foods, on must check for the word "Yashan" on the label. (Some *hechsherim* may be very small, appearing after the ingredients on the back and aren't always on the front.)

OU (Union of Orthodox Jewish Congregations of America

OK (The Organized Kashrus Laboratories)

Star-K of Baltimore

Rabbi Weissmandl

Rabbi Shlomo Stern (The Debrecener Rav)

Beit Din of New Square

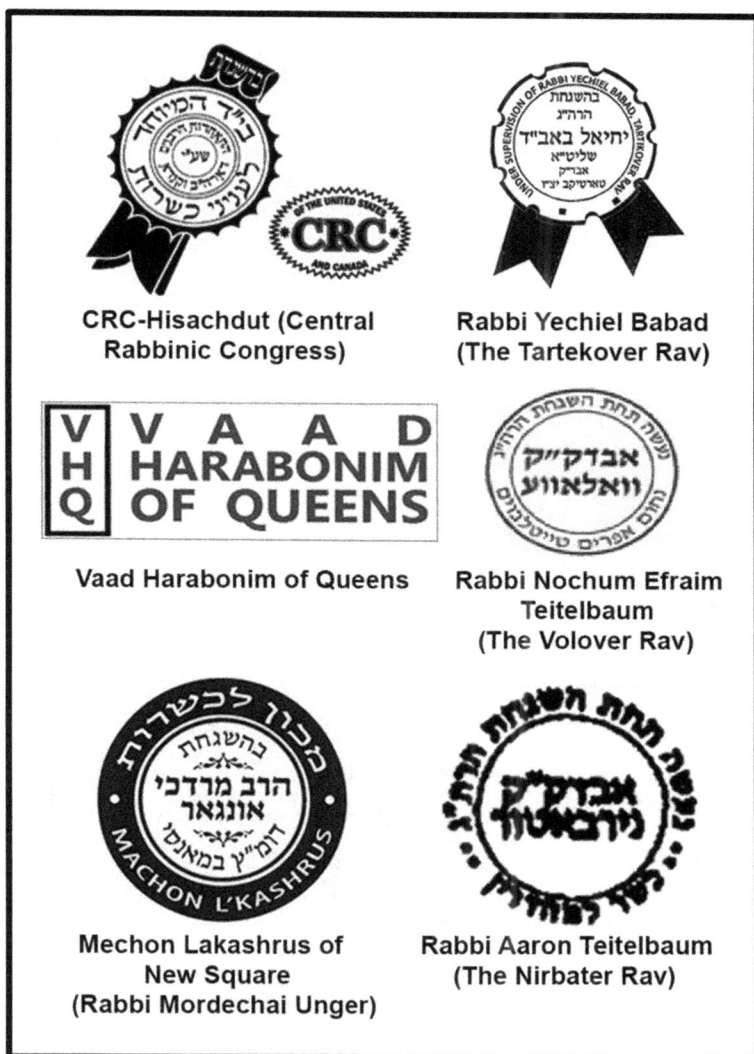

CRC-Hisachdut (Central Rabbinic Congress)

Rabbi Yechiel Babad (The Tartekover Rav)

Vaad Harabonim of Queens

Rabbi Nochum Efraim Teitelbaum (The Volover Rav)

Mechon Lakashrus of New Square (Rabbi Mordechai Unger)

Rabbi Aaron Teitelbaum (The Nirbater Rav)

As of the writing of this book, all pictured *hechsherim* had *yashan hashgacha* in one form or another, as mentioned. These are the most commonly seen symbols for these particular agencies, although some may have more than one *hechsher* design.

Hechsherim Where Malt Status Has Not Been Checked, and Are Yashan, Only with "Yashan" on the Label: If you hold that malt is *batul*, the *hechsherim* below are perfectly "always-*yashan*" for you. If you *do not* hold that malt is *batul*, you must always check the date codes on the packages bearing these *hechsherim*. All other ingredients are certified *Yashan*, however. "Yashan", "Yoshon", or "ישן" has to appear on the label to qualify.

Kof-K

cRc (Chicago Rabbinical Council

KAJ (K'hal Adath Jeshuran)

Rabbi Binyomin Gruber

Kehilah Kashrut (Flatbush Community Kashrut Organization)

Other Items Concerning Yashan Hashgacha: How do companies alternate between *chadash* and *yashan* runs? Other agencies may vary, but the OU policy for *yashan* is that a company either has equipment used exclusively for *yashan*, or it goes through a type of purging. In the latter case, just as for *kashering*, equipment must not have been used with *chadash* for over 24-hours. It is then flushed out with an already-*yashan* ingredient. That ingredient batch is then marked "Chadash", and any subsequent batches are considered *yashan*.

What about restaurants? When it comes to restaurants, catering, and kosher events, one must make sure that there is *yashan hashgacha* there too. *Mashgichim* must check all ingredients coming into the kitchen to make sure they're *yashan* as well as kosher. Knowledgeable kosher chefs won't cook or bake *yashan* items with *chadash* items, or the whole batch becomes *chadash*. Much goes into these that the consumer never sees. A local *kashrut* agency can tell you which places are *yashan* certified and those that aren't.

Rye, is a Winter crop in the USA and Canada. However, products like Rye Bread are often combined with Wheat Flour. (See page 25.)

Fresh-Baked Goods usually become Yashan later in the Western USA than in the East. (See page 85.)

Some flavored Potato Chips can contain Wheat and may be a problem. (See page 29.)

Gefilte Fish and some other items are made with Winter Wheat and always are Yashan! (See pages 26 and 32.)

Chapter 4

History of Packaged Foods

Yashan, Kosher and Other Food History: There is quite a history to keeping *yashan*. Back in the Biblical era when grain was stored and then ground into fresh flour, it was a simpler time. Since all Jews kept *yashan*, all the Five Grains were stored up until the next *Pesach* when the *Omer* was brought to the Temple. It was pretty straightforward, store the grain and then use it. However, when a person used this grain, they knew exactly what went into the foods they were making. There was not very much to keep track of.

Things didn't change much until the start of the Industrial Revolution in Great Britain in the middle of the 1700s. From there, industry spread out, eventually making its way to the USA and the rest of Europe.

During the 1800s, steam engines were invented, as well as new modes of transportation. Machinery was developed, and with it so did new manufacturing processes. This would eventually lead to a lack of consumer knowledge of what went into packaged food products. (What exactly *are* we eating?)

Let's take a trip through time...

Late 1800s: A Jewish Food Revolution!

Just after the Civil War in the late 1800s, the "Second Industrial Revolution" came about, with the spread of electric power, cross-country transportation of foods by rail, and factories featuring mass-production including of course, commercially-produced foods. Society gradually moved from agrarian to urban. The "general store", stocked with barrels and bins of bulk items that were weighed-to-order, gradually changed to shelves full of colorful pre-packaged foods. It was a new concept in buying food, and many Jewish companies joined this revolution.

1868: The Fleischmann Brothers opened the very first commercial yeast-making plant. They revolutionized baking with their "compressed yeast" and later inventions like "Rapid-Rise" yeast.

1869: Dr. Brown's Cel-Ray Tonic was invented and sold in every Jewish New York deli. Dr. Brown's later expanded to other flavored sodas as well.

1870: Rokeach started manufacturing kosher soap. To appreciate this, one must realize that originally soap was made from a mixture of lye and lard or other usually non-kosher fats. Not a good thing to wash your kosher dishes in! They later increased their company's product line to include gefilte fish, jams and soups in the early 1900s.

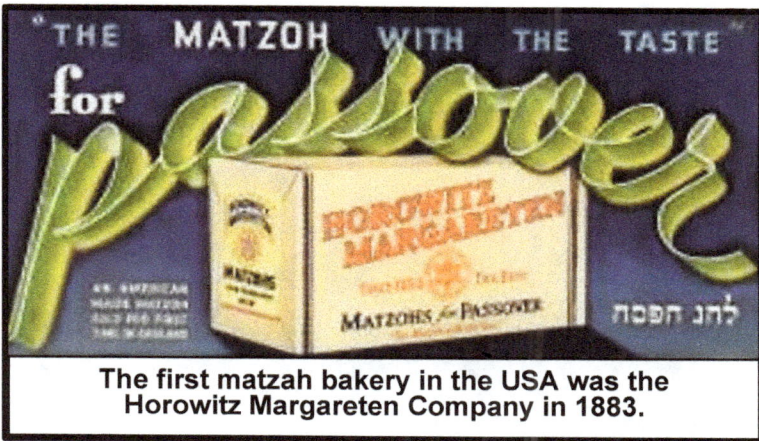

The first matzah bakery in the USA was the Horowitz Margareten Company in 1883.

1883: The first matzah bakery to open in the USA was the Horowitz Margareten Company on the Lower East Side of Manhattan. In 1923, an amazing and pious woman, Regina (Horowitz) Margareten was one of few businesswomen to have a managerial position in those days. Hailed as the "Matzah Queen", she basically ran the company until just before her death at age 96 in 1959.

1887: The Manischewitz Company was founded in Cincinnati, Ohio. By 1900, they produced 50,000 pounds of matzah per day and shipped it around the world. In 1912, Manischewitz invented square machine-made matzah. It later acquired Horowitz Margareten.

1889: Although not Jewish, one of the first companies to make pre-packaged mixes was Aunt Jemima. Eventually, the company did target new Jewish immigrants, selling kosher *latke* mixes in the 1930s-1940s. With a spokeswoman posing as Aunt Jemima, they had ads entirely in Yiddish, as seen below.

Aunt Jemima came out with some of the first complete mixes in 1889. They sold latke mix in the 1930s- '40s as seen in an ad in Yiddish.

1898: Fifty Orthodox congregations join forces to become the Union of Orthodox Jewish Congregations of America, better known as the "OU". It was created to help preserve the traditional Orthodox Jewish way of life.

The Early 1900s: Packaged Foods Abound!

1906: The Kellogg's company, (first called the "Battle Creek Toasted Corn Flake Company") was started. Corn flakes were originally produced for patients in the sanitarium run by the Kellogg brothers, who were Seventh-Day Adventists. They practiced a generally "kosher", vegetarian-based diet.

Strangely, many of Kellogg's cereals have only a "K" on the box. Over the years, these were actually certified by the KVH, (the Rabbinical Council of New England), which is known to be a reliable *kashrut* agency. Quite recently, the OU started doing *hashgacha* on many Kellogg cereals. They oversee most cereals, except for "Unfrosted Mini Wheats", (possibly due to shared equipment, as the "Frosted Mini Wheats" contain gelatin made from non-kosher beef). As an interesting side note, marshmallows in Kellogg's cereals contain gelatin derived from pork, and the Kellogg brothers would not have eaten them!

Kellogg's Corn Flakes ad in *Life* magazine, July 21, 1910.

In the mid-1900s, the kosher consumer didn't have much to rely on in the way of food product labeling. The first federally-enforced law, the Pure Food and Drug Act of 1906 was passed in an effort to prevent misleading or false statements on labels. It did not mandate displaying actual ingredients on product labels.

The 1910s: Metal cans as we know them today became popular. End disks rolled together with the main can and sealed under pressure replaces the old canning process of soldering together the ends with lead-based tinning. In 1908, the H.J. Heinz Company also came out with the "enameled tin", which helped prevent corrosion.

1911: A non-Jewish mainstream company, Proctor and Gamble produced Crisco in 1911, a kosher shortening made entirely of vegetable oils instead of animal fat. It helped revolutionize baking *parve* [non-meat or dairy] desserts for the Jewish household.

1913: The Gould Amendment assured that labels displayed the proper package quantity of products, although mandatory listing of ingredients on food labels was still not yet instituted.

1915: The New York State Legislature passed the first-ever Kosher Food Law, prohibiting non-kosher food to be fraudulently sold as kosher food. It also required stores selling kosher foods to post signs stating that they were.

1916: Aron Streit founded a business in New York's Lower East Side of Manhattan, originally making matzah by hand.

1916 also saw the opening of "Piggly Wiggly", the first self-service grocery store. It didn't sell perishables, so the independent general store, local butcher shop, and milkmen delivering to homes still prevailed.

The 1920s: The OU's new kosher certification department was started in the 1920s. However, the first product wouldn't have certification until three years later.

1923: The very first commercially-produced food to ever bear an OU *hechsher* was H.J. Heinz Company's vegetarian baked beans in 1923. The need for *hashgacha* became blatantly obvious, as Heinz had originally produced four different types of baked beans, three of which contained pork.

Not Pessachdig!

| HEINZ Cream of Mushroom Soup | HEINZ Cream of Asparagus Soup | HEINZ Cream of Tomato Soup | HEINZ Cream of Celery Soup | HEINZ Cream of Green Pea Soup | HEINZ Cream of Spinach Soup |

The Ⓤ on the labels of these products and 46 other Heinz varieties does not mean that they are Pessachdig. The Ⓤ means that they contain no meat and no fat.

The Ⓤ means that the Union of Orthodox Jewish Congregations of America certifies these articles—but for year round use. Not for Passover.

HEINZ Oven Baked Beans

HEINZ Tomato Ketchup

We wish you a Happy Passover! We'll be with you when the holidays are over.
H. J. Heinz Co.   Pittsburgh, Pa.

The first product to be kosher-certified is Heinz vegetarian baked beans in 1923. They are shown here with other items in this clever ad from 1937.

Also in '23, Maxwell House became the first certified "Kosher for Passover" coffee, and later in 1932 produced the famous annually-printed *Maxwell House Haggadah*.

An original 1923 ad in Yiddish for Maxwell House, the first ever certified "Kosher for Passover" coffee. Their famous Haggadah came 9 years later.

1927: Lender's bagel bakery was founded in New Haven, Connecticut by Harry Lender. Later in 1962, Lender's had the first operational bagel machine, enabling the commercial production of frozen bagels.

Packaged baking mixes appeared now and then in the 1920s and '30s, mostly for pancakes. P. Duff & Sons came out with the very first "complete cake mix".

The original cake mixes already had the eggs in the mix, and all one had to do was add water, mix it and bake. It actually didn't go over very well, because housewives were so accustomed to making cakes from scratch that they felt like they weren't really doing anything. My how times have changed! (That same cake mix would probably sell very well in our busy lives of carpools and cellphones today.) Unfortunately, spoilage was still a big problem, as packaging was not perfected yet, so the next wave of (eggless) cake mixes wouldn't become popular for another few decades in the 1950s.

NOW- Just a bowl and a spoon..

to make your favorite cake!

SOUNDS incredible, doesn't it? But that's all you need. A bowl and a spoon . . . and a package of Duff's Cake Mix of your family's favorite type! Just empty the Mix into your bowl . . . add water . . . stir well . . . and the batter's ready for the oven! Here's the modern way, the easy way, to make delicious cakes. Try it . . . to save you time and trouble, and to give your family a real taste treat! P. Duff & Sons, Inc., Pittsburgh, Pennsylvania.

Ginger Bread
Spice Cake
Devil's Food
White Cake

DUFF'S CAKE MIX

The first cake mix is made by P. Duff & Sons in 1939-1940.

The 1930s: In 1929, Clarence Birdseye watched the Inuit of Northern Canada preserving their food with ice, wind, and sub-zero temperatures. This gave him a great idea. In August of 1930, he patented a "Quick Freeze" machine, and introduced the world to the concept of "flash freezing". Soon after, he came out with his own line of "frosted foods" including meats, vegetables, fruits and seafood. Retailers and consumers alike were reluctant at first, not wanting to invest in expensive freezers.

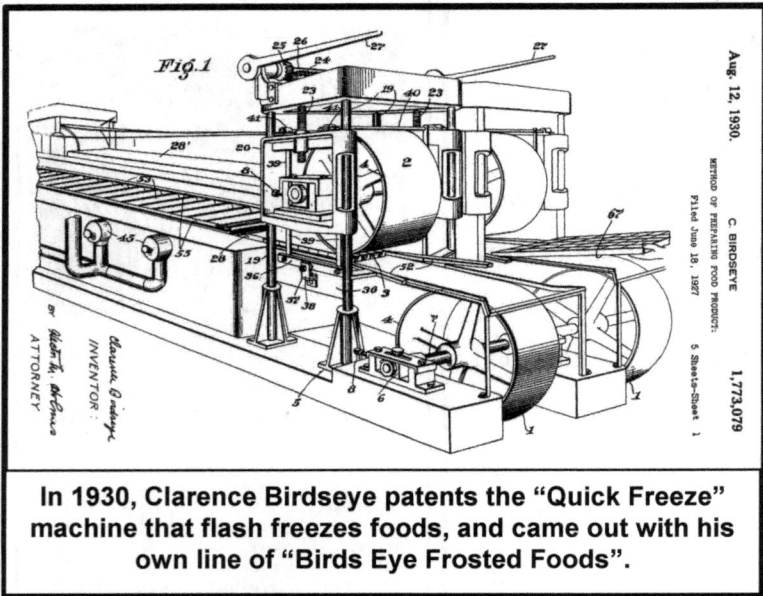

In 1930, Clarence Birdseye patents the "Quick Freeze" machine that flash freezes foods, and came out with his own line of "Birds Eye Frosted Foods".

Frozen foods became popular in the institutional market. Surplus frozen foods were utilized for steamship and railroad clientele. The passengers did not know that the foods had been frozen before their preparation. It could easily be disguised, and then be served just like fresh food and the hungry travelers would be none the wiser.

The first true supermarket chain "King Kullen" opened in 1930 in Jamaica, Queens, in New York City. For the first time ever, this store offered perishables, meat and dairy, along with packaged foods all in one convenient place, and it even had a surrounding parking lot for cars. After this, many larger grocery store chains opened up. Shopping for food would never be the same.

1933: Proctor and Gamble, the makers of *parve* Crisco shortening, regularly targeted the Jewish consumer. Knowing that they had a good market, they offered a cookbook that was in Yiddish and English.

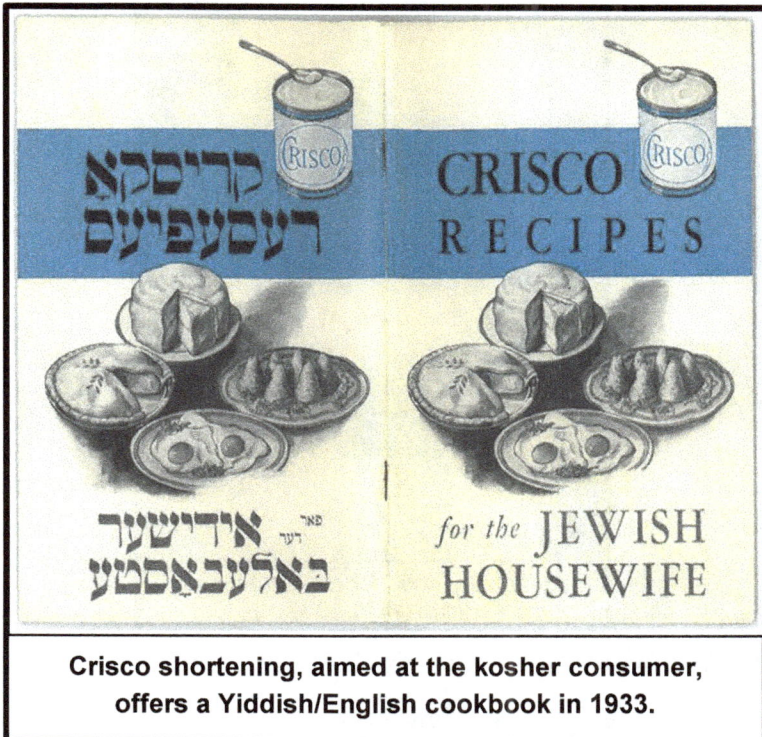

Crisco shortening, aimed at the kosher consumer, offers a Yiddish/English cookbook in 1933.

1934: Up until now, Monarch Wine Company originally made "legal" sacramental and ritual wine. Now that Prohibition ended, they leased the Manischewitz name to put on their bottles, and borrowed Manischewitz' *mashgichim* as well. "Manischewitz" (Monarch) is now the largest maker of kosher fruit wines.

1937: After 45 years of its existence as a company, one of the most advertised products of all-time, Coca-Cola finally becomes kosher-certified in the USA, due to merely changing its source of glycerin. Coke doesn't generally display a *hechsher*, but they are currently under the *hashgacha* of the OU.

After 45 years, Coca-Cola goes kosher in 1937.

1938: Empire Kosher Poultry, Inc. was started by the Katz family in the Catskills, New York.

Also, in '38, the Food Drug and Cosmetics Act was finally passed, mandating ingredients on product labels. Before then, consumers were not able to really know what products were kosher or even contained the Five Grains.

৪০ে৪০ে

The Time of World War II

HOW TO SHOP WITH WAR RATION BOOK TWO
... to Buy Canned, Bottled and Frozen Fruits and Vegetables; Dried Fruits, Juices and all Canned Soups

YOUR POINT ALLOWANCE MUST LAST FOR THE FULL RATION PERIOD
Plan How Many Points You Will Use Each Time Before You Shop

BUY EARLY IN THE WEEK   BUY EARLY IN THE DAY

A 1943 war poster issued by the government teaches how to purchase rationed packaged foods.

When WWII came about, the rationing of metals took its toll on canned goods, and suddenly frozen foods were cheaper. The government was trying to develop a product to supply soldiers with a good amount of vitamin C to help try to prevent scurvy. Their highly-acidic lemon drink crystals just didn't hit the spot for thirsty soldiers, and instead it was preferred for use as a floor-cleaning agent. Just after the war ended, vitamin C-packed frozen-concentrated orange juice was developed, and it became a very popular item.

Thankfully, for those who kept *yashan*, all domestic surplus wheat in the USA was stored. From the 1930s through the 1950s, there was no worry about *chadash* wheat.

1948: Back in 1948, Czechoslovakian winemaker Eugene Herzog moves to the USA. The Herzog family winery was well known for being the royal wine supplier to the emperor of the Austro-Hungarian Empire. He renamed the new family business "the Royal Kedem Wine Corporation".

The 1950s: Easy-to-prepare foods with longer shelf life were originally developed by the military for war rations with innovations like cellophane packaging. After the war, many commercial food companies had leftover factories that were utilized for what have now become modern "convenience" foods.

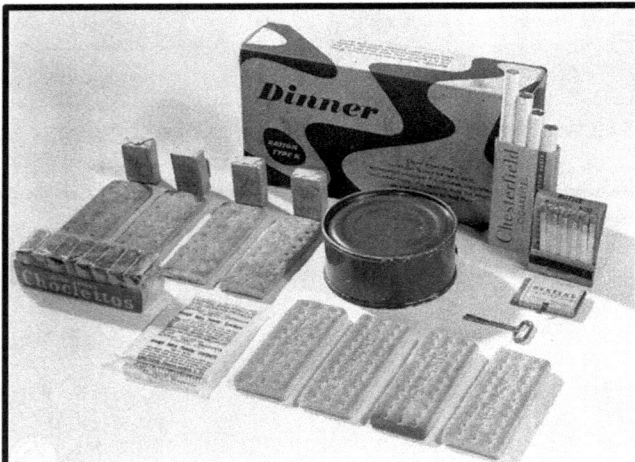

During WWII, processed foods started being made for war rations, and the highly-acidic powdered lemon drink crystals (front at left of crackers) were more preferred to be used as a floor-cleaning.

Back in the 1950s, powdered eggs were no longer added to cake mixes and they became a best-seller! Now the housewife could feel proud that she went to the extra trouble to add eggs to her cakes. As populations started spreading out into the suburbs, most food was still proudly made from scratch. The new "Television Age" was ushered in, and along with it, frozen foods became even more popular with new inventions like "TV dinners" and fish sticks.

1957: Rav Aaron Soloveitchik, a strict adherent to *yashan*, became the *kashrut* supervisor for Streit's matzah. Later he learned that not all flour was *yashan*. He helped found the first North American *yashan* bakery in Chicago, Illinois.

The 1960s: As times changed, so did food processing. More women started having careers and working outside the home. With the popularity of TV and other social factors, time became of the essence. Life got faster and "instant foods" grew increasingly popular.

1962: Frozen kosher meals were now offered on airplane flights. They were made by Lou G. Segal's, a Manhattan kosher restaurant. The Segal's airline meals division was later bought out by Milton's. Soon after, caterer Sam Borenstein came onto the scene making airline meals for El Al airlines, and Julius Schreiber pioneered frozen kosher meals that were flown anywhere around the world. Alle Processing later acquired Schreiber's. Alle Processing produces the *yashan* "Meal Mart" dinners as well as other frozen foods. They provide kosher meals to hospitals as well as airlines.

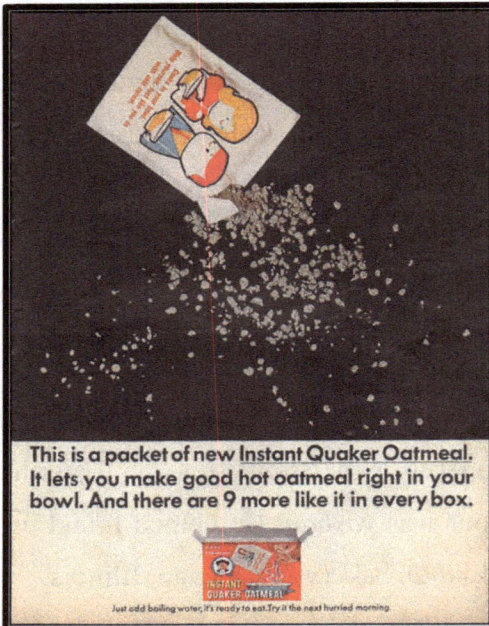

This is a packet of new **Instant Quaker Oatmeal.** It lets you make good hot oatmeal right in your bowl. And there are **9** more like it in every box.

Just add boiling water, it's ready to eat.Try it the next hurried morning.

Quaker Instant Oatmeal is introduced to the world in 1966.

Microwaves came out in the mid-1950s, but consumer countertop-sized ovens came out in 1967.

1966: The Quaker Oats Company introduces instant oatmeal packets to the world. The first flavor, "Maple and Brown Sugar" came out in 1970.

1967: Developed in the 1940s from radar technology during the war, the first home-use microwaves were sold in the mid '50s (like the 1956 Westinghouse microwave at left), but they were big and expensive. In 1967, the very first Amana countertop microwave oven, the "Radarange", was introduced.

1970s- The Start of the Yashan Revolution

Microwave ovens started becoming popular in the '70s. This helped to increase the sale of frozen foods, and enabled people to fix a frozen meal within minutes. Working women were now commonplace after the recession. Now more than ever there was the need for pre-packaged instant foods.

With convenience foods on the rise, it was increasingly more difficult to know what foods were *yashan*. What was even worse is that the USA started selling all their surplus wheat to Russia, and there no longer were the *yashan* stores to rely on for those who kept the *mitzvah*.

1972: With the pending *yashan* wheat crisis looming, Rabbi Yoseph Herman stepped in to keep track of the status of grains in the USA. Back then, he would contact various manufacturers about their products, and calculate the status from using dates supplied by the companies. What originally started as a list for a few careful *yashan*-keepers quietly keeping the *mitzvah*, bloomed over time into a full-time job for Rabbi Herman with Project Chodosh and the annual publication, "A Guide to Chodosh".

Over time, he could no longer rely on information from manufacturers and contacted the USDA for crop data. Since then, *A Guide to Chodosh* has become the "bible" of *yashan*-keeping as it remains today. A subscription for one year originally had three printed issues with updates that were mailed. They were later offered via email in a pdf as well.

Throughout these lean years of the '70s, *yashan* flour was kept in limited supply, usually in cold storage. There was a large risk involved by the companies who did this. Not only were they concerned about their flour not selling, but the constant threat of bug infestation was always a reality.

***The 1980s*:** Kemach Food Products Corp. was founded in Brooklyn, New York. It was the first company committed to making several *yashan* products, and is presently supervised by Rabbi N.N. Horowitz. They produce *yashan* flour and many *parve*-only products, shipping all over the world. They make all information about their products' *yashan* status easily available on their website, and even have their own *yashan* email list for those who want to receive updates.

1987: Kosher food is now in vogue! Data tracking agency Lubicom Marketing Consulting, started a kosher-certified food trade show for venders, companies and consumers that was held at the Jacob K. Javits Convention Center in New York. With a capacity crowd of over 50,000 people, another 50,000 others showed up but were not allowed to attend. It blossomed into what has become a two-day annual event called "Kosherfest". Currently, it is held on a Tuesday and Wednesday every November at the Meadowlands Exposition Center in Secaucus, New Jersey. Only those in the kosher food industry can attend. It is no longer open to the public.

The 1990s: The '90s saw the addition of many mainstream non-Jewish companies requesting kosher certification.

1990: After 120 years of packaged kosher food products in the USA, 1990 saw the introduction of the first ever "Federal Kosher Consumer Bill" to protect consumers against fraud.

1999: The kosher food industry has over 7 million consumers, and there are only 2 million who are Jewish. Kosher food sales top $4 billion, growing more each year.

Also in 1999, Walmart starts to cater to the kosher consumer. A store was even opened in the Catskills, New York. Most Walmart stores have at least a small kosher section in the ethnic foods aisle, with a fairly nice selection of assorted "Jewish" brands. Many of the Walmart "Great Value" products are kosher, and can be found throughout the store.

ဆဝ္ဆဝ

2000- The New Turn of the Century

The turn of the century saw even more kosher food growth. There was much more interest in *yashan* foods as well. More and more companies become *yashan*-aware.

2009: In response to the growing number of *yeshivot* [religious schools for boys and men] that were interested in keeping *yashan*, there was a major joint-venture between ConAgra Foods and the Kof-K certification agency to produce *yashan* flour in their Denver plant. This would ensure a steady supply of *yashan* flour. A *mashgiach* [kosher supervisor] was continually on-site for packing and sealing the railroad cars for transport. A *mashgiach* would also be on-site at the receiving Bronx ConAgra plant to clean and seal the trucks after packing, ready to distribute the flour.

The 2010s: There are now a reported 9 million kosher consumers and growing, spending over $40 billion on kosher-certified foods.

2011: Yoshon.com was created to offer direct downloads of the *Guide to Chodosh* and to report product information online obtained from the *Guide* for those who had internet access. This filled a niche that Project Chodosh was not allowed to pursue, due to an anti-internet *p'sak* that was given. That *p'sak* has been faithfully honored throughout the years.

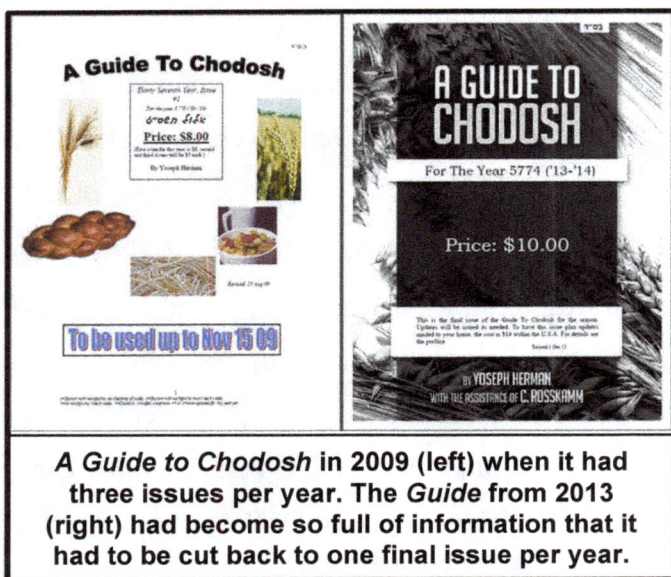

A Guide to Chodosh in 2009 (left) when it had three issues per year. The *Guide* from 2013 (right) had become so full of information that it had to be cut back to one final issue per year.

2013: *A Guide to Chodosh* was streamlined to just one *Preliminary Guide* with one final complete *Guide* coming out just after the holiday of *Sukkot*. Before and during the main issues, there are updates on the status of products.

2014: A new non-profit organization called "The Yoshon Network Inc." (TYNI), was created, which was unaffiliated with Project Chodosh. The Yoshon.com website was transferred to TYNI, and in 2016 the site was greatly improved for use on mobile devices enabling *yashan* consumers to look up products more easily in stores as they were shopping. It also allowed visitors to download

The *Yoshon.com* website as of 2016, on a mobile device for use in stores as people shop for food.

the *Guide to Chodosh, Chodosh Bulletin Updates*, and view pictures of the products along with any *yashan* updates reported from the *Guide*. It later offered news updates and the *yashan* status of products from *kashrut* agencies around the world.

With a growing awareness of *yashan*, and more companies offering gluten-free products, the *mitzvah* of keeping *yashan* should inevitably keep getting easier and become more wide-spread.

Oatmeal Creme Cookies. Mmm,
but Oats are the first of all the
crops to become Chadash!
(See pages 27 and 35.

Bread made with "Sprouted Grain"
Flour after the second day of Pesach.
Is it a problem? (See pages 40-42.)

It may be surprising to find out that
there are Oats in your Gluten-Free
Veggie Burger and Barley in your
Tea Bags. (See page 27.)

Chapter 5
Determining Yashan Status

How Does It Work? Sometimes it's possible to determine a product's status on your own. If you look at the *General Cut-Off Dates* chart in Chapter 2, it gives a good idea of how determining *yashan* status works. Every year, the USDA reports when the crops are harvested, then the general *chadash* dates are published. As information comes in, the dates are confirmed. If one knows the best by date and a product's shelf life, this can determine what the original packing date was, which in turn will reveal whether a product is *yashan* or not. One need only compare the packing date to the *chadash* cut-off date of the grains in the product's ingredients.

If a package has a date, it can be a packing date or best by date. Most commercial products such as 25-50 lb. sacks of flour have packing dates. Consumer products like 1-10 lb. bags of flour usually have best by dates. How do you tell which is which? If a date has passed, it's a packing date. If it's in the future, it's a best by date. What if there's only a series of letters or numbers? Once deciphered, it usually reveals the packing date.

The main factor for a cut-off date is the grain ingredient. Each grain is harvested at a different time. If a product has multiple grains, it's date is determined by the grain with the earliest cut-off date. Now let's learn how to figure it all out!

Where to Find the Date Codes

Date codes can be ink-stamped or embossed on packages. Every product must have one somewhere. On perishables like bread or frozen dough, it can either be printed on the bag itself or on a "Kwik Lok" tab holding the package shut, as above.

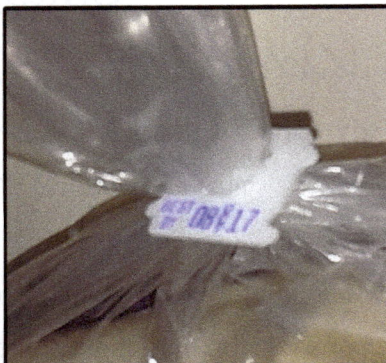

The only time date codes are truly hidden, is in the case of boxes containing individually-wrapped items like Nature Valley Granola Bars. It's important to know to check the date code on the individual bar wrappers inside and *not* the (often different) date on the box! This is specified in the *Guide*.

Dates embossed on the end of paperboard boxes, as with pasta, can be very hard to find. If you have trouble seeing them, take the package and hold it up in bright light so that there's a glossy reflection. The date will usually show up as a slight shadow. Sometimes that's the only way to see them.

Looking head-on (left), an embossed date code can be nearly invisible on the box, until it is turned slightly (right) to to see a subtle shadow in reflected light.

Packing Date and Purchase Date

Two dates appear in the *Guide's* General Start Dates, packing date and purchase date. What are they? Let's dispel the confusion:

Packing Date: This is the date on which a product was packaged. It is always accurate to determine *yashan* status. I recommend for newcomers to stick with using the packing date or date code on most products. It's always consistent.

Purchase Date: Purchase dates are later than packing dates. They are hypothetical dates estimating when products will be *chadash* by the time they are purchased. They can be useful for perishable, freshly-baked items with limited shelf life, and a date closer to harvest. Purchase dates for freshly baked items are also region-specific, and they're fine for items like bread. Although for other less perishable items, purchase dates just make things more confusing in an already challenging task of figuring out a product's status.

My rationale for stating that purchase dates aren't as accurate for non-freshly baked items is simple: Not all purchase dates are created equal! Here's why...

First, if a store is high-priced, its products don't sell as fast and may be older (a real advantage for *yashan*-keepers). Another factor is when a store buys a lot of extra stock and warehouses it, which can also cause dates to be later.

Most people like deals, so stock at a lower-priced store sells quickly. Therefore, the dates at a cheaper store will always be newer.

The other reason is timing differs due to travel duration in the USA. I was amazed at how late some products arrive in the west compared to the east. Let's see an example as to how it works (or how "purchase dates" don't work as well).

A factory produces wheat crackers in Indiana on August 2nd. (The date on the boxes are Aug 2.) They are sent to a store in Ohio, taking 2 days to get there. Crackers from the same lot are also sent to California. Their transit time takes two weeks. In two weeks' time, all the August 2 crackers at the Ohio store were sold. The Ohio store now has a new shipment of crackers on their shelves made August 14th. Meanwhile in California, the August 2nd batch of crackers finally arrives and is put on the shelves. An Ohio man finds the wheat crackers at his store with a date of Aug 14. That same day in California, a woman finds the wheat crackers, but at her store there is a packing date of Aug 2. The wheat *chadash* cut-off date is August 9th, so the California lady's crackers are still *yashan*! The guy in Ohio sees his crackers are Aug 14, which is *after* August 9th. His crackers are *chadash*, so he sadly puts the crackers back and walks away.

The above is so true! In the West, I still found *yashan* frozen dough around *Purim*! In the East, this was *chadash* by January or earlier, although most products aren't quite this unusual. If someone in the West were to go by the purchase date, many "still-*yashan*" items may be missed out on.

How Date Codes Started

Surprising as it may sound, there is no Federal regulation in the USA for date codes. The only exception is that the FDA does require Food Product Dating on infant formulas. A few states have guidelines or local laws which seem to come and go. Date codes in the USA are pretty much left up to the individual manufacturer as to what they feel it should be. Governments in many other countries actually do regulate Food Product Dating, such as the UK, Canada, Hong Kong, and the European Union.

The history of the date code is quite interesting. Back in mid-1931, Alphonse Gabriel Capone, who is better known as the famous gangster Al Capone, decided to buy a milk-processing company called "Meadowmoor Dairies". Wanting to get into a more legitimate business,

Al Capone in 1931, a few months before he lobbied to pass a law in Chicago requiring expiration dates to be visibly stamped on milk bottles.

he was already set for bottling drinks from being in the bootleg business, so why not? His brother Ralph, nicknamed "Bottles", was the one who thought of putting visible expiration dates on the milk bottles. Al then lobbied for, and succeeded in, getting the Chicago City Council to pass a law for mandatory date-stamping on milk. The passing of this legislation helped him take over the milk industry in Chicago. This is perhaps the first instance of Food Product Dating ever recorded. Although he was arrested and convicted for income tax evasion only three months later, who would have thought that we would have Al Capone to thank for introducing the main source of determining if

Original Lucky Lager beer can from 1935.

many of our foods are *yashan*!

Two years after Prohibition ended in 1933, General Brewing Company produced "Lucky Lager" beer in 1935. It was the first "age dated" beer to have a "Brewed Before Date" stamped on the can. This enabled people to tell when it had been produced, and ensured that it had been aged properly. Now consumers could physically see that they weren't buying "green beer", or beer that is bitter and too "young". Since then, the American brewing industry has had "freshness dating", but it didn't really become popular until 1985. It's still not legally mandated, and has more to do with sales publicity than food safety.

Not much happened with product date codes until the 1960s. Kroger of Cincinnati, Ohio started regularly added dates to their pasteurized milk packages to help prevent spoilage. With the advent of highly processed foods in the late 1960s and early '70s, customers wanted to know that their food was fresh. By 1973, over 60 retail supermarkets had some form of dating on their products in response to consumer demand, *not* consumer safety.

Here is an excerpt from the USDA's website, which displays their general concept of dating systems:

> *"USDA estimates food loss and waste at 30 percent of the food supply lost or wasted at the retail and consumer levels. One source of food waste arises from consumers or retailers throwing away wholesome food because of confusion about the meaning of dates displayed on the label. To reduce consumer confusion and wasted food, FSIS* [Food Safety and Inspection Service] *recommends that food manufacturers and retailers that apply product*

dating use a "Best if Used By" date. Research shows that this phrase conveys to consumers that the product will be of best quality if used by the calendar date shown. Foods not exhibiting signs of spoilage should be wholesome and may be sold, purchased, donated and consumed beyond the labeled "Best if Used By" date."

In another place on the same page it says, "Confusion over the meaning of dates applied to food products can result in consumers discarding wholesome food." Actually, they do have a good point, because there is a *mitzvah* in the Torah to not be wasteful called, "Bal Tashchit". It is found in *Devarim* 20:19-20 and describes the prohibition of destroying fruit trees during a war (see page 24). This law extends to wasting anything, from smashing an object in anger to throwing away perfectly good food.

Indeed, date codes and Food Product Dating can be very confusing, perhaps due to it not being government regulated. The FDA recommends a "best if used by" date, but often manufacturers have their own system and don't want to change. It's compounded by retailer belief that consumers will search for the newest dates, leaving old stock on the shelves. (The opposite of what *yashan*-keepers do.) Grocers routinely rotate their stock so this (ideally) won't happen.

Throughout the years, stores had a system of "closed dating". Inventory was tracked internally by coding known only to them, and the public had no knowledge of it. In the early 1970s, "open dating" was required by several states, which displayed regular Gregorian (secular) calendar dates on packaging in the form of "sell by" or "best by". This trend continues, but is still only enforced on a state or local level.

Date codes can be listed in a variety of ways. In order to fully comprehend how to decipher what products are *yashan*, we need to understand them.

౿౮ఁ౿౮ఁ

The Different Date Code Systems

These can be displayed in different ways, but they are still the key to learning about the *yashan* status of a product.

Closed Dates: These are date codes known only to the manufacturer, consisting of numbers, letters, or often a combination of both. They can be deciphered with the help of the *Guide*. The manufacturer explains the code, reports the code for that product's cut-off date, and its explanation is listed in the *Guide*. On rare occasions, there may be a limited *yashan* run, and only this batch's code numbers are listed.

Open Dates: These are ordinary dates on the Gregorian calendar. It can be a packing, best by, sell by, use by, or a suggested expiration date. Usually, it's in a Month/Day/Year format, although some companies are going to the European style of dating as a Day/Month/Year format. Months can be written by assigned number (January=1), spelled out, or abbreviated. See the examples on page 94.

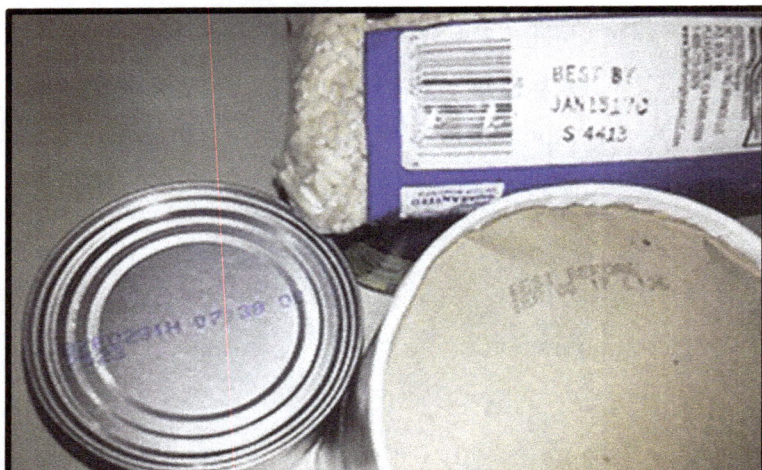

A bag of barley (top right) states, "Best By Jan 15 17". An oatmeal container (lower right) lists, "Best Before Sep 06 17". Both of these are examples of "Open Dating", and are pretty straightforward.

A can of beef barley soup (lower left) exhibits "Closed Dating", a code known mainly to the retailer and manufacturer. The important part of the code is "231H", meaning Aug. 18, 2018. The "231" is the Julian Date for Aug. 18th. H = 8 in alpha-numerical code, or "2018".

Julian Dates: These can be listed in different ways, but are the actual number of the days throughout the year. January 1=001, December 31=365. Best known for use on egg cartons, they can be used on any product. One or two-digit years are listed first or last with the day number. The date above is, "August 18, 2018". August 18th is the 231st day of the year, so it can also be listed "8231" or "2318", "18231" or "23118", depending on the company.

How to Read Various Date Codes

We need to learn this to determine when a product was made. Later, we'll learn about shelf life. We already learned about the *chadash* cut-off dates. Together these three elements are needed to figure out a product's status.

For closed dates, the *Guide* may list the number series, or say the first few numbers are unimportant. Using the can on the previous page, the code is "87ED231H 07:38 OU". It may be listed in the *Guide* as "packing date is XXXX231H (XXXX=unimportant, 231=Aug. 18, H=8 in alph. order)".

For open dates, it can go by either of the two different calendars. Gregorian dates are the most common, the *Guide* may list a general secular or Gregorian calendar date. It may be listed as "best by 08/18/2018" for a product. Pretty obvious, it means August 18, 2018. Other ways to list the same date could be "Aug 18 18", "08-18-18", "18 Aug 18". They may or may not be preceded by "best by", "best if used by" or "sell by". Some packages have only a date on them.

For Julian dates, numbers before 100 could be read without the zeros in the beginning (001=1, 026=26) but it is unlikely. Most go by three digits. It's important to note that numbers are different during a leap year. Since each day is a number, an extra day throws the system off by one. (What a difference a day makes!) To discern Julian dates, see the handy charts on pages 95-100.

Other Dates and Codes: Months or years can be expressed alphabetically by letters or numerically by numbers. The *Guide* lists alternatives. Below are samples...

Months as Alphabetical Codes		Abbreviated Month Codes in the USA		Canadian Bilingual Month Codes	
Month	Letter	Month	Letters	Month	Letters
January	A	January	JAN	January	JA
February	B	February	FEB	February	FE
March	C	March	MAR	March	MR
April	D	April	APR	April	AL
May	E	May	MAY	May	MA
June	F	June	JUN	June	JN
July	G	July	JUL	July	JL
August	H	August	AUG	August	AU
September	I	September	SEP	September	SE
October	J	October	OCT	October	OC
November	K	November	NOV	November	NO
December	L	December	DEC	December	DE

Months as Numbers		Years as Letters		Years as Numbers	
Month	Number	Year	Letter	Year	Number
January	01 or 1	2011	A	2011	1
February	02 or 2	2012	B	2012	2
March	03 or 3	2013	C	2013	3
April	04 or 4	2014	D	2014	4
May	05 or 5	2015	E	2015	5
June	06 or 6	2016	F	2016	6
July	07 or 7	2017	G	2017	7
August	08 or 8	2018	H	2018	8
September	09 or 9	2019	I	2019	9
October	10	2020	J	2020	0
November	11				
December	12				

Starting on the opposite page are Julian calendar charts. Numbers for the dates during normal years are shown in the blue charts, and for leap years they're in the green charts.

Julian Dates Chart for MOST YEARS (Usually is for Packing Dates)							
Day	Date	Day	Date	Day	Date	Day	Date
001	Jan 1	031	Jan 31	061	Mar 2	091	Apr 1
002	Jan 2	032	Feb 1	062	Mar 3	092	Apr 2
003	Jan 3	033	Feb 2	063	Mar 4	093	Apr 3
004	Jan 4	034	Feb 3	064	Mar 5	094	Apr 4
005	Jan 5	035	Feb 4	065	Mar 6	095	Apr 5
006	Jan 6	036	Feb 5	066	Mar 7	096	Apr 6
007	Jan 7	037	Feb 6	067	Mar 8	097	Apr 7
008	Jan 8	038	Feb 7	068	Mar 9	098	Apr 8
009	Jan 9	039	Feb 8	069	Mar 10	099	Apr 9
010	Jan 10	040	Feb 9	070	Mar 11	100	Apr 10
011	Jan 11	041	Feb 10	071	Mar 12	101	Apr 11
012	Jan 12	042	Feb 11	072	Mar 13	102	Apr 12
013	Jan 13	043	Feb 12	073	Mar 14	103	Apr 13
014	Jan 14	044	Feb 13	074	Mar 15	104	Apr 14
015	Jan 15	045	Feb 14	075	Mar 16	105	Apr 15
016	Jan 16	046	Feb 15	076	Mar 17	106	Apr 16
017	Jan 17	047	Feb 16	077	Mar 18	107	Apr 17
018	Jan 18	048	Feb 17	078	Mar 19	108	Apr 18
019	Jan 19	049	Feb 18	079	Mar 20	109	Apr 19
020	Jan 20	050	Feb 19	080	Mar 21	110	Apr 20
021	Jan 21	051	Feb 20	081	Mar 22	111	Apr 21
022	Jan 22	052	Feb 21	082	Mar 23	112	Apr 22
023	Jan 23	053	Feb 22	083	Mar 24	113	Apr 23
024	Jan 24	054	Feb 23	084	Mar 25	114	Apr 24
025	Jan 25	055	Feb 24	085	Mar 26	115	Apr 25
026	Jan 26	056	Feb 25	086	Mar 27	116	Apr 26
027	Jan 27	057	Feb 26	087	Mar 28	117	Apr 27
028	Jan 28	058	Feb 27	088	Mar 29	118	Apr 28
029	Jan 29	059	Feb 28	089	Mar 30	119	Apr 29
030	Jan 30	060	Mar 1	090	Mar 31	120	Apr 30

Day	Date	Day	Date	Day	Date	Day	Date
121	May 1	152	June 1	183	July 2	214	Aug 2
122	May 2	153	June 2	184	July 3	215	Aug 3
123	May 3	154	June 3	185	July 4	216	Aug 4
124	May 4	155	June 4	186	July 5	217	Aug 5
125	May 5	156	June 5	187	July 6	218	Aug 6
126	May 6	157	June 6	188	July 7	219	Aug 7
127	May 7	158	June 7	189	July 8	220	Aug 8
128	May 8	159	June 8	190	July 9	221	Aug 9
129	May 9	160	June 9	191	July 10	222	Aug 10
130	May 10	161	June 10	192	July 11	223	Aug 11
131	May 11	162	June 11	193	July 12	224	Aug 12
132	May 12	163	June 12	194	July 13	225	Aug 13
133	May 13	164	June 13	195	July 14	226	Aug 14
134	May 14	165	June 14	196	July 15	227	Aug 15
135	May 15	166	June 15	197	July 16	228	Aug 16
136	May 16	167	June 16	198	July 17	229	Aug 17
137	May 17	168	June 17	199	July 18	230	Aug 18
138	May 18	169	June 18	200	July 19	231	Aug 19
139	May 19	170	June 19	201	July 20	232	Aug 20
140	May 20	171	June 20	202	July 21	233	Aug 21
141	May 21	172	June 21	203	July 22	234	Aug 22
142	May 22	173	June 22	204	July 23	235	Aug 23
143	May 23	174	June 23	205	July 24	236	Aug 24
144	May 24	175	June 24	206	July 25	237	Aug 25
145	May 25	176	June 25	207	July 26	238	Aug 26
146	May 26	177	June 26	208	July 27	239	Aug 27
147	May 27	178	June 27	209	July 28	240	Aug 28
148	May 28	179	June 28	210	July 29	241	Aug 29
149	May 29	180	June29	211	July 30	242	Aug 30
150	May 30	181	June 30	212	July 31	243	Aug 31
151	May 31	182	July 1	213	Aug 1	244	Sep 1

Day	Date	Day	Date	Day	Date	Day	Date
245	Sep 2	276	Oct 3	307	Nov 3	338	Dec 4
246	Sep 3	277	Oct 4	308	Nov 4	339	Dec 5
247	Sep 4	278	Oct 5	309	Nov 5	340	Dec 6
248	Sep 5	279	Oct 6	310	Nov 6	341	Dec 7
249	Sep 6	280	Oct 7	311	Nov 7	342	Dec 8
250	Sep 7	281	Oct 8	312	Nov 8	343	Dec 9
251	Sep 8	282	Oct 9	313	Nov 9	344	Dec 10
252	Sep 9	283	Oct 10	314	Nov 10	345	Dec 11
253	Sep 10	284	Oct 11	315	Nov 11	346	Dec 12
254	Sep 11	285	Oct 12	316	Nov 12	347	Dec 13
255	Sep 12	286	Oct 13	317	Nov 13	348	Dec 14
256	Sep 13	287	Oct 14	318	Nov 14	349	Dec 15
257	Sep 14	288	Oct 15	319	Nov 15	350	Dec 16
258	Sep 15	289	Oct 16	320	Nov 16	351	Dec 17
259	Sep 16	290	Oct 17	321	Nov 17	352	Dec 18
260	Sep 17	291	Oct 18	322	Nov 18	353	Dec 19
261	Sep 18	292	Oct 19	323	Nov 19	354	Dec 20
262	Sep 19	293	Oct 20	324	Nov 20	355	Dec 21
263	Sep 20	294	Oct 21	325	Nov 21	356	Dec 22
264	Sep 21	295	Oct 22	326	Nov 22	357	Dec 23
265	Sep 22	296	Oct 23	327	Nov 23	358	Dec 24
266	Sep 23	297	Oct 24	328	Nov 24	359	Dec 25
267	Sep 24	298	Oct 25	329	Nov 25	360	Dec 26
268	Sep 25	299	Oct 26	330	Nov 26	361	Dec 27
269	Sep 26	300	Oct 27	331	Nov 27	362	Dec 28
270	Sep 27	301	Oct 28	332	Nov 28	363	Dec 29
271	Sep 28	302	Oct 29	333	Nov 29	364	Dec 30
272	Sep 29	303	Oct 30	334	Nov 30	365	Dec 31
273	Sep 30	304	Oct 31	335	Dec 1		
274	Oct 1	305	Nov 1	336	Dec 2		
275	Oct 2	306	Nov 2	337	Dec 3		

Julian Dates Chart for LEAP YEARS (Usually is for Packing Dates)							
Day	Date	Day	Date	Day	Date	Day	Date
001	Jan 1	031	Jan 31	061	Mar 1	091	Mar 31
002	Jan 2	032	Feb 1	062	Mar 2	092	Apr 1
003	Jan 3	033	Feb 2	063	Mar 3	093	Apr 2
004	Jan 4	034	Feb 3	064	Mar 4	094	Apr 3
005	Jan 5	035	Feb 4	065	Mar 5	095	Apr 4
006	Jan 6	036	Feb 5	066	Mar 6	096	Apr 5
007	Jan 7	037	Feb 6	067	Mar 7	097	Apr 6
008	Jan 8	038	Feb 7	068	Mar 8	098	Apr 7
009	Jan 9	039	Feb 8	069	Mar 9	099	Apr 8
010	Jan 10	040	Feb 9	070	Mar 10	100	Apr 9
011	Jan 11	041	Feb 10	071	Mar 11	101	Apr 10
012	Jan 12	042	Feb 11	072	Mar 12	102	Apr 11
013	Jan 13	043	Feb 12	073	Mar 13	103	Apr 12
014	Jan 14	044	Feb 13	074	Mar 14	104	Apr 13
015	Jan 15	045	Feb 14	075	Mar 15	105	Apr 14
016	Jan 16	046	Feb 15	076	Mar 16	106	Apr 15
017	Jan 17	047	Feb 16	077	Mar 17	107	Apr 16
018	Jan 18	048	Feb 17	078	Mar 18	108	Apr 17
019	Jan 19	049	Feb 18	079	Mar 19	109	Apr 18
020	Jan 20	050	Feb 19	080	Mar 20	110	Apr 19
021	Jan 21	051	Feb 20	081	Mar 21	111	Apr 20
022	Jan 22	052	Feb 21	082	Mar 22	112	Apr 21
023	Jan 23	053	Feb 22	083	Mar 23	113	Apr 22
024	Jan 24	054	Feb 23	084	Mar 24	114	Apr 23
025	Jan 25	055	Feb 24	085	Mar 25	115	Apr 24
026	Jan 26	056	Feb 25	086	Mar 26	116	Apr 25
027	Jan 27	057	Feb 26	087	Mar 27	117	Apr 26
028	Jan 28	058	Feb 27	088	Mar 28	118	Apr 27
029	Jan 29	059	Feb 28	089	Mar 29	119	Apr 28
030	Jan 30	060	Feb 29	090	Mar 30	120	Apr 29

Day	Date	Day	Date	Day	Date	Day	Date
121	Apr 30	152	May 31	183	July 1	214	Aug 1
122	May 1	153	June 1	184	July 2	215	Aug 2
123	May 2	154	June 2	185	July 3	216	Aug 3
124	May 3	155	June 3	186	July 4	217	Aug 4
125	May 4	156	June 4	187	July 5	218	Aug 5
126	May 5	157	June 5	188	July 6	219	Aug 6
127	May 6	158	June 6	189	July 7	220	Aug 7
128	May 7	159	June 7	190	July 8	221	Aug 8
129	May 8	160	June 8	191	July 9	222	Aug 9
130	May 9	161	June 9	192	July 10	223	Aug 10
131	May 10	162	June 10	193	July 11	224	Aug 11
132	May 11	163	June 11	194	July 12	225	Aug 12
133	May 12	164	June 12	195	July 13	226	Aug 13
134	May 13	165	June 13	196	July 14	227	Aug 14
135	May 14	166	June 14	197	July 15	228	Aug 15
136	May 15	167	June 15	198	July 16	229	Aug 16
137	May 16	168	June 16	199	July 17	230	Aug 17
138	May 17	169	June 17	200	July 18	231	Aug 18
139	May 18	170	June 18	201	July 19	232	Aug 19
140	May 19	171	June 19	202	July 20	233	Aug 20
141	May 20	172	June 20	203	July 21	234	Aug 21
142	May 21	173	June 21	204	July 22	235	Aug 22
143	May 22	174	June 22	205	July 23	236	Aug 23
144	May 23	175	June 23	206	July 24	237	Aug 24
145	May 24	176	June 24	207	July 25	238	Aug 25
146	May 25	177	June 25	208	July 26	239	Aug 26
147	May 26	178	June 26	209	July 27	240	Aug 27
148	May 27	179	June 27	210	July 28	241	Aug 28
149	May 28	180	June 28	211	July 29	242	Aug 29
150	May 29	181	June 29	212	July 30	243	Aug 30
151	May 30	182	June 30	213	July 31	244	Aug 31

Day	Date	Day	Date	Day	Date	Day	Date
245	Sep 1	276	Oct 2	307	Nov 2	338	Dec 3
246	Sep 2	277	Oct 3	308	Nov 3	339	Dec 4
247	Sep 3	278	Oct 4	309	Nov 4	340	Dec 5
248	Sep 4	279	Oct 5	310	Nov 5	341	Dec 6
249	Sep 5	280	Oct 6	311	Nov 6	342	Dec 7
250	Sep 6	281	Oct 7	312	Nov 7	343	Dec 8
251	Sep 7	282	Oct 8	313	Nov 8	344	Dec 9
252	Sep 8	283	Oct 9	314	Nov 9	345	Dec 10
253	Sep 9	284	Oct 10	315	Nov 10	346	Dec 11
254	Sep 10	285	Oct 11	316	Nov 11	347	Dec 12
255	Sep 11	286	Oct 12	317	Nov 12	348	Dec 13
256	Sep 12	287	Oct 13	318	Nov 13	349	Dec 14
257	Sep 13	288	Oct 14	319	Nov 14	350	Dec 15
258	Sep 14	289	Oct 15	320	Nov 15	351	Dec 16
259	Sep 15	290	Oct 16	321	Nov 16	352	Dec 17
260	Sep 16	291	Oct 17	322	Nov 17	353	Dec 18
261	Sep 17	292	Oct 18	323	Nov 18	354	Dec 19
262	Sep 18	293	Oct 19	324	Nov 19	355	Dec 20
263	Sep 19	294	Oct 20	325	Nov 20	356	Dec 21
264	Sep 20	295	Oct 21	326	Nov 21	357	Dec 22
265	Sep 21	296	Oct 22	327	Nov 22	358	Dec 23
266	Sep 22	297	Oct 23	328	Nov 23	359	Dec 24
267	Sep 23	298	Oct 24	329	Nov 24	360	Dec 25
268	Sep 24	299	Oct 25	330	Nov 25	361	Dec 26
269	Sep 25	300	Oct 26	331	Nov 26	362	Dec 27
270	Sep 26	301	Oct 27	332	Nov 27	363	Dec 28
271	Sep 27	302	Oct 28	333	Nov 28	364	Dec 29
272	Sep 28	303	Oct 29	334	Nov 29	365	Dec 30
273	Sep 29	304	Oct 30	335	Nov 30	365	Dec 31
274	Sep 30	305	Oct 31	336	Dec 1		
275	Oct 1	306	Nov 1	337	Dec 2		

Why Do I Need to Know About "Shelf Life"?

Shelf life is the "average life expectancy" for food. When there is no packing date, there will be a date indicating the estimated end of a food's shelf life, (the "best by date"). As mentioned earlier in "How Date Codes Started", there is no federal regulation for this in the USA. It is left up to each manufacturer as to how long they feel that their product will still be at its peak freshness. Therefore, a company stamps a suggested date on the product, such as, "best by June 8, 2018". Contrary to popular belief, it doesn't mean that it expires right then on that date and any time after that date it will have gone bad. These dates are simply estimates, and food generally lasts far longer, provided it has been stored properly. Shelf life is part of the key to finding out if certain products are *yashan*.

The shelf life of a product is the amount of time that the manufacturer thinks its product remains wholesome. It is different for every product. A bag of seasoned potato chips may have a shelf life of several months, whereas a box of spaghetti can have a shelf life of up to 3 years. This determines the date code, which is the shelf life after packing. Therefore, if the pasta has a shelf life of 3 years and it was packed on August 1, 2017, it's date code will be 3 years after the packing date, and shall be listed as "best by August 1, 2020". The BBQ potato chips were packed on that same day somewhere else, but their shelf life is only 3 months. That means their "best by date" will be on November 1, 2017. The best by date is always determined by the shelf life assigned to it by the company. The shelf life will be listed in *Guide to Chodosh* as so many days or months "after packing". This helps one retroactively find out what date their product was actually packed, and if it is before the "chadash cut-off date", it's *yashan*! A date listed in the *Guide* is the "*chadash* cut-off date" for the product, meaning that this exact date is when the product becomes *chadash* and is no longer permitted. Any dates before that cut-off date are always *yashan*. It should be noted that *yashan* reports are the opposite in other countries. The "*yashan* date" is reported, (not a "*chadash* date"), meaning that a product with *that date or earlier is yashan.*

Most of the time, the shelf life remains the same for that product every year. Unless a company changes ingredient formulas, or simply decides to change the timing for some reason, this is usually pretty consistent in the "world of *yashan* foods". Most often, the average spaghetti has a 3-year shelf life, egg noodles a 2-year shelf life, and perhaps the majority of cold cereals and all-purpose flours a 1 or 2-year shelf life. These vary with company, but it's a general guide for common products. The most common need for this is in the *Guide's* "Quaker/Mother's Chart". It lists all cereals under their shelf life. The consumer must look at a cereal's ingredients to determine from the chart which is the cut-off date. Some product shelf-life listings have the exact number of days. If you see "(558 days after packing)" in the *Guide*, that's the shelf life.

Knowing the shelf life comes in handy when a year and date are so similar that it is hard to determine an actual date. For example, a product has a date of 18 JUL 19. Is it July 18, 2019 or July 19, 2018? Usually, the year will be listed last, but if you know the shelf life of the product is 6 months, and you just purchased it a few days ago on January 25, 2018, you'll then know that the actual date has to be July 19, 2018.

ಬುಲಜಬುಲಜ

Factory and Mill Codes

Often there will be factory or mill codes to identify where a product was made. This can be vital to knowing if a product is *yashan* or not. For instance, the Gold Medal factory in Kansas City only produces their all-purpose and bread flours from winter wheat. Therefore, they put "KC" as part of the date code. The other Gold Medal factories make flour with *chadash* spring wheat.

Sometimes the *Guide* lists mill codes as two letters. If it's important to report a mill code to know *yashan* status, it is listed. If not, it will usually be listed as something like "AA" or "XX". These are just "placeholders" so to speak, letting one know that two letters will appear there. If this is the case, it will usually be listed as "XX=unimportant".

Test Your Knowledge of Date Codes!

Hopefully, the previous sections have given you all you need to determine the *yashan* status of packaged foods.

When one learns something new that is crucial to their life, it's always a good idea to take a quiz to see how well they understand it. The following exercise is great for those who enjoy math puzzles or if you simply want to make sure you "know your stuff". The following quiz compares products (all names have been changed) with *yashan* date code info. (Warning, some may be trick questions!)

You're looking at *Guide to Chodosh*, comparing *Guide* info (**G**) to your package (**P**). Answer yes (Y) or no (N) to the questions. Bonus points to those who can answer why!

1. **G**: *TaysT Puff Pastry Sheets Code: 7211T (7=year, 211=day of year, T=unimportant).*

    P: It is 2016. On your package, it has a date code of **N7214**. (Is it *yashan*—Y or N?)

2. **G**: *So-Gud Healthy Grains Cereal (1 year after packing) the date code is July 23 19.*
    P: It is 2018. Your box says **July 19, 2019**, and it contains oats, wheat and barley malt. The cut-off date for oats is July 20th, the wheat cut-off date is August 7th and barley is August 5th. (Is it *yashan*—Y or N?)

3. **G**: *So-Gud Bran Cereal (1 year after packing) code: Aug. 18 19.*

   P: It is 2018. Your box says **Aug 15, 2019**. It contains wheat and barley malt. The wheat cut-off date is August 18, barley cutoff date is August 14. (Is it *yashan*—Y or N?)

4. **G**: *Fluffy-Lite BBQ Potato Snax (6 months after packing) date code: 12/12/17.*

   P: It is 2017. Your bag has wheat flour in it and says **1/24/18**. (Is it *yashan*—Y or N?)

5. **G**: *Dr. Hooke Breaded Fish Sticks (18 months after packing) Code: 03620.*

   P: It is 2019. Your box contains wheat and malt, the code is **23019**. (Is it *yashan*—Y or N?)

6. **G**: *Howdy Seasoned Beef Jerky: best before 2018 SEP 28 (6 months after packing).*

   P: Behold! Your package says best before **2018 SEP 28**. (Is it *yashan*—Y or N?)

7. **G**: *Pot-Luck Spicy Fries Code: 7211 (7=year, 211=day of the year. The code is preceded by "L" or by "LOT"). Ignore the "best by" date.*

   P: The bag says "best used by **July 31, 2017** and it also has **LOT7197**. (Is it *yashan*—Y or N?)

Quiz Questions 8-10. The *Guide* has a chart for the Shaker company since they make so many cereals. Your objective is to look at the chart and discern the cut-off date.

    G. *There are 2 different shelf lifespans- 180 days and 240 days. Dates for oat items with 180-days is Jan 22 16 and for 240-days is Mar 22 16. Dates for wheat items with 180-days is Jan 29 16 and 240-days is Mar 29 16.*

Shaker Cereals Chart				
Days	**Oats Date**	**Wheat Date**	**Barley Date**	**Malt Date**
180	Jan 22 16	Jan 29 16	Jan 27 16	Jun 15 16
240	Mar 22 16	Mar 29 16	Mar 27 16	Aug 14 16

8. **P.** You have a box of Shaker Fun Flakes. It contains wheat and oats. In the *Guide's* "Shaker Chart", the Fun Flakes shelf life is 240 days. Your box says Mar 25 16. (Is it *yashan*—Y or N?)

9. **P:** Shaker Pops, 240-days with wheat only. Your box is Mar 23 16. (Is it *yashan*—Y or N?)

10. **P.** Shaker Rings, 180-days, with oats only. Your box is Dec 27 15. (Is it *yashan*—Y or N?)

(Quiz answers are at the end of *Resources* on pages *154-155*.)

Chapter 6
Diving into Vintage Grain

Starting to Keep Yashan: Where Do I Begin?

First, make sure you think you can do it. Remember the three "Ps"– "Plan, Practice, and Put-away". Take the questionnaire on pages 43-44. Decide what you can spend, where you can get items, and how or where to store them. You will need to put aside enough for about six to seven months. Start stocking up early on items that aren't readily available. Figure out what you use the most of. It's all a matter of planning ahead.

For some, it is helpful to designate a certain area of the house to keep their store of *yashan* items. If you have the room, a freezer is a good idea. If space is an issue, remember that a small chest freezer can also be utilized as a table, or a buffet shelf to serve food on. It can be covered with a decorative cloth or some contact paper to be prettier and disguise it. Other ideas are to purchase large plastic bins for storage. Often refrigerators just aren't quite enough.

If you live in a city with a large Jewish population, you may not have to worry about stocking up. As stated before, it depends highly on where you live. If you do opt to buy and store items, please read the storage tips throughout pages 112-115. Some of these tips can prevent a lot of heartache later on.

When to Start

Without a doubt, the easiest time to start keeping *yashan* is just after *Pesach*. You will be in great company. Although not well known, the wife of the noted Rabbi Eliezer Silver would buy 150 pounds of flour after *Pesach* to ensure a store of *yashan* flour for her *challot* throughout the whole year.

Everything (with perhaps the exception of fresh or frozen "sprouted-grain" bread) is *yashan,* so you have plenty of time to "Plan, Practice and Put-away". When *yashan* season is ending and *chadash* products are starting to hit the shelves, it's usually late summer to early fall, around *Rosh Hashana* or *Sukkot* depending on how late it falls that year. When *chadash* season is early it's a bit harder. Fortunately, there are sales in late summer as stores want to clear out old stock. There are also sales for Memorial Day in the USA.

৪০৫৪০৫

Making it Through Your First Year

It is extremely beneficial to befriend the buyer for a small food store or a manager in the grocery section of a supermarket. They can assist and advise you. I had an amazing experience with a manager who sincerely liked helping his customers. I explained about how *yashan* worked, and he was fascinated. Being Catholic, he also felt religious values were important, and he truly respected it. He went out of his way to help, telling me what items would be on sale and the times for the best sales. One year, he kept ordering extra crackers for me from his supplier that were on sale but hadn't come in. The supplier kept sending the wrong size. To top it all off, when the correct ones came in, he actually gave me two cases of the crackers for free, because I was "such a patient customer". At first, I turned him down, but he insisted! I'm sure this is rather rare, and I think he retired a few years later, but the point is, it helps immensely to have a contact in the business.

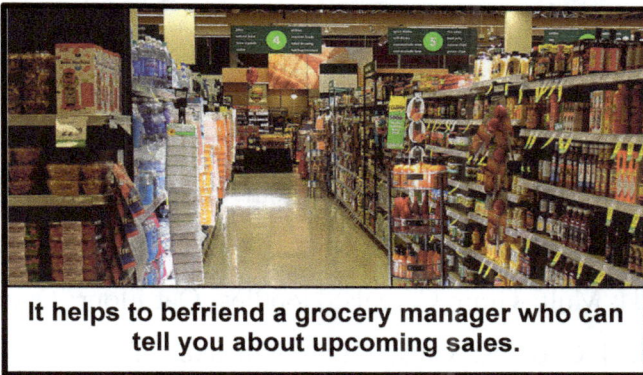

It helps to befriend a grocery manager who can tell you about upcoming sales.

Planning Ahead

For the first "P", one must plan out the year. Just like *Shabbat* and holidays, there is the element of planning-ahead. You will want to estimate what foods to get, and how much you and your family will eat. Take an average of what is eaten per week or month, and multiply it out so that you have a store of at least six to seven months. Don't forget to take into account anything that guests might request, or items that you may want to make as gifts for others. It never hurts to slightly overestimate.

These are some products you may want to stock up on:

Appetizers; Baby Foods; Bagels; Bagel Chips; Barley for Soups and Cholent; Barley-Water Drinks; Beer; Blintzes; Bread; Bread Crumbs; Breaded Frozen Foods; Brownie Mix; Buns; Burritos & Wraps; Cake Mixes; Cakes; Candy (with Wafers); Cereals; Chocolate Malt Syrup; Cholent Mixes; Chow Mein Noodles; Cookies; Cornflake Crumbs (can contain Malt); Couscous; Crackers; Crepes; Crisped Rice Cereals (usually contain Malt); Croutons; Doughnuts; Egg Rolls; Egg Roll Wrappers; Fish Sticks; Flour; Flour Tortillas; Frozen Doughs and Crusts; Granola Bars; Hors D'euvres; Ice Cream (with Dough or Pretzels); Knishes; Malted Milk Balls; Malted Milk Shakes; Multi-Grain Breads; Multi-Grain Cereals; Noodles, Oat Flour; Oatmeal; Oatmeal Cookies; Oats; Orzo; Pancakes; Pasta; Pastries; Pearled Barley; Pie Crusts; Puffed Pastry Sheets; Pies; Pita Bread; Pita Chips, Pizza; Pretzels; Rice Mixes; Rolled Oats; Rye (if imported), Rye Bread; Rye Crackers; Snacks; Soup Mixes; Soups in Cans, Cartons or Frozen; Spelt or Spelt Bread (if imported); Spicy Fries; Stuffing Mixes; Tea (if flavored); Vegan Products (most contain Wheat Gluten); Vital Wheat Gluten; Wafers; Waffles, Wheat Berries; Wheat Flour; Whole Wheat Bread; Whole Wheat Flour; Won Ton Wrappers.

Substitutions for the Five Grains

The second "P", experience or "Practice", is invaluable. If you run out of an item or can't find *yashan* products, here are some substitutions for foods made from the Five Grains.

Since anything not containing the Five Grains are automatically considered "yashan", there are many products to choose from. Look into items made for *Pesach* as they are great substitutes. It may be helpful to investigate "gluten-free" foods, but be sure to check the ingredients for oats.

Substitute Items for Products Made of the Five Grains			
Wheat	**Oats**	**Barley**	**Malt**
Grits or Teff for Creamy Wheat Cereal	Buckwheat Groats for Oatmeal	White Rice for Barley in Soup	Root Beer for Malt Soft Drink
Quinoa or Millet for Couscous	Amaranth for Oatmeal	Brown Rice for Barley Dishes	Maple Syrup for Malt Syrup
Matza Sheets for Lasagna Noodles	Quinoa or Buckwheat for Oats	Red Rice for Barley Dishes	Red Wine Vinegar for Malt Vinegar
Arrowroot, Corn Starch, Potato Starch as Flour for Thickening	Ground Nuts for Oat Crumb and Cobbler Toppings	Quinoa for Barley Dishes	Popped Amaranth for Puffed Rice Cereals
Potato Starch Noodles for Pasta	Millet for Oatmeal		Cocoa with Coffee for Malted Milk
Rice for Orzo Pasta	Brown Rice for Oatmeal		
Soy or Rice Flour for Wheat Flour	Teff for Oatmeal		
Ground Nuts and Margarine for Wheat Pie Crust	Amaranth Flour for Oat Flour		

Buying and Storage Tips

Our last of the three "Ps" is to store or "Put-away". Even though *yashan* foods are older, staleness is usually not a problem. As mentioned, get acquainted with a manager who can inform you on upcoming sales or can order extra items.

Check for products in the back of the shelves. You would be surprised at how many workers ignore the rules and don't rotate the stock. (Their "laziness" is to our benefit!)

Once you plan ahead and know what to get, it's easier. When looking to buy products, look for airtight plastic bags by squeezing them slightly. Airtight bags act like balloons. It helps keep food fresh and bugs out for long-term storage.

It is better to get pasta in bags than boxes. Sometimes paper attracts pests and they can enter through cracks, which we will talk more about in the next section. Products, such as barley, rice and beans come in ventilated bags. They must be stored in a refrigerator or airtight bags. Self-sealing zipper bags are better than those with a separate zipping mechanism.

More tips on buying and storing foods can be found in the next section about dealing with bugs. Bug prevention is also part of the process of choosing what to buy, (or more specifically, what to look for) and most importantly, how to select items when buying your precious *yashan* stash for the coming *chadash* season. Since it is an investment, you want to make sure that everything is well-protected.

What You Don't Want to Know, But Should

Nearly every *yashan* article I read talks about food "developing worms". Don't freak out over this, it is really more of a descriptive term, referring to bugs in general. They are not true worms, like earthworms that live in soil. The largest "worms" found in food are actually the larvae of various species of Meal Worm Beetles, often used as food for fish, birds and reptiles. They are commonly found in grain storehouses or fields and are separated out during processing. Other smaller "wormy-looking" larvae are usually inside grain and not often seen. Other pupae encase themselves in cocoons or webbing as they grow. We will look mainly at what are called "pantry pests", which are most commonly found in homes and grocery stores.

Now for the "gross" facts. Most food products have microscopic bug eggs in them. It is part of the natural order of things, no different than when we breathe the air which is filled with dust and microbes. *Halachically*, anything too small to see with the naked eye is not a problem. Even when checking vegetables for bugs, it does not have to be done with a magnifying glass or jeweler's loupe. This is the whole reason that *Halachically*, microscopic bug eggs are allowed to be consumed. This is true for parts of a bug as well. It's less of a problem to unknowingly consume a bug part, but to eat a whole non-kosher insect is a severe problem! Which brings us to this- the USDA has a manual called *Allowable Food Defects*, outlining rules for amount of eggs and bug parts allowed in foods. (Not a pleasant read!) Fortunately, eggs won't hurt us and we don't realize they are there. Knowing this comes the answer to, "How did bugs get into my food?" They were there already and simply hatched. Grains are infested at the field where they grew or in the storehouse. Bugs enter packages or lay eggs in bag seams and box flaps. Follow the tips below to keep foods bug-free...

✿ When shopping: Visually inspect grocery shelves and packages you buy. Avoid anything that appears to have webbing or little brown flaky things, which are often molted skins from growing pests.

✿ Pay attention! Look for anything crawling, even as tiny as a period, or small moths flying around.

✿ Watch for powder where an item was sitting. If there's an excessive amount of powder in barley, or in the bottom of boxes, it can be evidence of bugs having eaten.

✿ Look for airtight packaging. Avoid any packaging with small round holes, as these are likely pests that chewed through to get inside. Bags of barley, rice or beans are often ventilated, so visually inspect their contents.

✿ Store creamy wheat cereals, barley and oatmeal in the refrigerator at all times.

✿ Put inner cereal bags (be careful, boxes can make holes) or flour in airtight plastic sealing bags. Label the bags with a permanent marker if needed for identification.

✿ Freeze items for at least 24-hours before putting them into bags or jars. This is handy for any grain product as well as seeds and rice. It helps kill any eggs that may be (and likely are) in your product.

✿ If you don't have an extra freezer, an alternative is to bake items to kill any eggs. Spread food out on a cookie sheet and put it in the oven at 150° F for two hours. Once the food cools, transfer it into well-sealing jars, containers, or good quality resealing airtight bags. These storage items can usually be reused.

✿ Keep pantry shelves clean and dust free. Although a little dust or crumbs in a cabinet may not seem like a big deal, they can be a substantial amount of food for tiny bugs looking for a meal.

✿ If food can't be stored in a freezer, put them in sealable plastic bags or large airtight containers. If you have a case of something, take it out of the cardboard box and store it in plastic bins.

✿ Perhaps the most important of all the above tips is to never store boxes of food on the floor. The ground is "bug habitat" only! (I learned this the hard way.)

Dealing with Infestations

No matter how clean a person is, tiny bugs can find their way into boxes or bags of food as early as at the warehouse or the grocery store. If you see just one bug crawling around on the counter, it may just be a straggler that came in from outside. However, if you see more than one of the same type, it's usually bad news. Identifying an infestation is pretty easy, sometimes it's just a matter of paying attention. If you see a bug in your food, that is the first, easiest sign. Other signs are not quite as obvious. Sometimes, you may not see any bugs, but the larvae could be laying-in-wait, hibernating in its pupal state as it gets ready to hatch into an adult. Unfortunately, if there are only eggs in the food, one cannot determine this until it's too late. If one catches an infestation in time before it spreads, it can save any other foods nearby. These are the signs of infested food:

✿ Clumps of food stuck together in little clusters, sometimes attached to a package.

✿ Food is stuck to packaging, sometimes being held in mid-air by tiny threads. These are silk threads made from caterpillars or larvae, hatched from eggs in the food.

✿ Dust and webbing along the top of food in the package.

✿ Tiny cocoons attached to corners of boxes, lids of jars, or corners of cabinets.

✿ Excessive powdery residue at the bottom of bags (or boxes) of food, and the bag is usually no longer airtight.

✿ Visibly eaten food, such as crackers with holes in them in unusual patterns. There may even be bugs inside.

✿ Little hairy looking balls distributed within the food. These are larvae just entering the pupal state.

✿ Tiny hairy caterpillars slinking along, looking for a place to start their hibernation.

✿ Brown scaly-looking skins that float if airborne. These are molted skins of Dermestid Beetles. If dispersed among food it's probably infested. If randomly appearing in a drawer, it's often not problematic.

✿ "Moving food". If food such as flour, oats or most especially creamy wheat cereals appears to be alive and moving, quickly but gently get the item out of the house and into a garbage. These are most likely Psocids, and they reproduce rapidly and infest quickly.

Hopefully, you will never need this information, but if you happen to get an infestation, here is what to do: Remove and inspect all foods from wherever they are stored, whether in cabinets, shelves or drawers. I am always amazed to find molted skins in silverware drawers when there is not even any food in them! Very carefully and slowly, take all infested foods and gently put them in a box or plastic bag and seal it up. Some pests are so small that if it is done too quickly, they can become airborne and land without even seeing it happen. Get it into a garbage can outside and as far away as possible. Vacuum the cabinets, shelves and drawers well to get any hidden eggs, bugs or molts out of the corners, and carefully get rid of the vacuum bag or contents outside. It can be helpful to wipe off other items in the cabinet. Wipe down the cabinet, shelf or drawer insides. Use bleach disinfectant sheets, or clean them thoroughly with a solution of half vinegar and half water. Some add peppermint oil to the solution to help repel future bugs. Once the areas are clean, open drawers or doors and let them air out a few hours. Remember, bugs love humidity, so storage areas must be as dry as possible before putting items back. Take precautions to prevent eggs from hatching before storage. It applies to all bug-prone foods like rice or nuts, not just the Five Grains.

જીભ્ભજીભ્ભ

Preventing Infestations

When it comes to preventing infestations, I personally do not like the idea of pesticides, especially in cabinets containing food. I prefer a more natural approach. If I see a spider in a cabinet or the kitchen I leave it there. Spiders are our friends, and they eat pantry pests. Other natural predators are wasps and certain flies that attack larvae, but these are out in the fields where bugs attack crops and grains.

Some storehouses release small parasitic wasps to take care of the problem, but this is on a larger scale. The major key to prevention is in the buying and storing of products, but there are some natural bug deterrents that may possibly help prevent

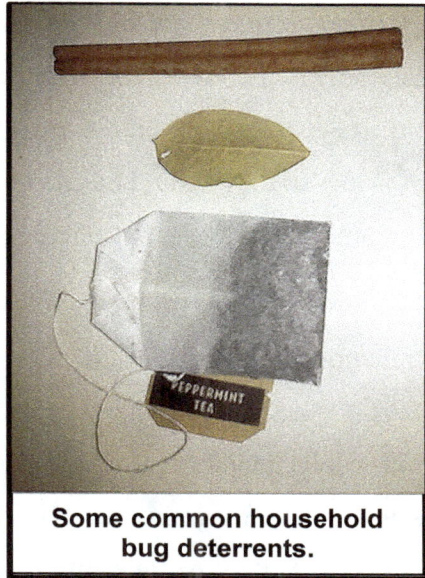

Some common household bug deterrents.

infestations from the outside. To ward off bugs, try placing some of these items in the corners of your food cabinets:

Common Household Items: Bay Leaves; Cedar Chips (bedding for pet rodents); Cinnamon Sticks; Eucalyptus Leaves (often found in dried flower arrangements); Peppermint Tea Bags.

Sprigs of Plants from Herb Gardens: Lavender; Mint; Rosemary; Tansy; Wormwood.

Natural Products: There are some bug traps made especially for pantry pests, called "Pheromone Traps", which reproduces the scent of the bug and draws them in, keeping them in the trap and away from foods. I have not tried these, but it is apparently a good alternative to pesticides.

Do note that these are not remedies to get rid of pests, they only help to repel them. Once the repellent items get too old they may lose their aromatic properties and stop working, so they should be changed periodically. There is no guarantee with these, but many people do use them.

Storing items properly is mainly the key to bug prevention more than anything else. Not only are bugs in food disgusting to think about, but even if they are removable, they can greatly degrade the quality of food. This is a problem in grain storehouses. Bugs contain moisture themselves, they excrete after eating, and rob the grain of their nutrients. All the more reason that grains are checked for quality before they even reach the manufacturer.

Make sure food items are stored in as cool of an area as possible. An attic or upstairs closet is not the best place to store food. A basement pantry is great if there is very little humidity. Bugs do not thrive when humidity is 50% or lower, as they need moisture to survive.

It can't be reiterated enough to store items in airtight jars, sealing containers or heavier zipper bags (without a separate zipping mechanism). Good quality bags can be reused, especially if only the inner bag or the contents of a boxed product is put inside. Keep outer bags airtight so bugs won't smell the food. Aggressive bugs chew holes in bags to enter if something smells good inside.

Bug ID

In order to keep products pest-free and staying fresh throughout the *chadash* season, one should learn more about them. ("Know your enemies!")

"Pantry pests", is a general term for bugs that inhabit food or grain items in kitchen cupboards, not other general living areas. Bugs such as roaches and silverfish may be at home in a house, but are not generally found in food.

Identifying grain pests is a helpful way to combat them. They can differ in appearance and sometimes their tastes for food. Pests found in the fields, or that feed on damaged, rotten or fungus-infested grains in storehouses aren't displayed. We will look at the most common pantry pests. There are thousands of species and it is impossible to include every single bug. Those within the same family that look similar will only be mentioned but not shown.

If you are not bothered by bug pictures and want to make sure any potential infestation outbreaks are containable, then it's worth your while to read on.

The following pages contain close-ups of many common pantry pests. They range from about half an inch long to 1/32nd of an inch. We will examine them going from the largest to the smallest. (Or might I say, the "creepiest"!)

Mealworm Beetles: These are most likely where the term comes from when referring to food becoming "wormy".

The largest of all the grain pests, the beetles are about half an inch long, and larvae can be about an inch long. Mealworm Beetles are native to the Northern USA and attack whole grains, the larvae feeding inside them. They are more commonly found in granaries and fields than in the kitchen pantry, but to get an idea of what is said by food becoming "wormy", the larvae of these are as close as they come. Larvae are commonly raised as pet food for fish, birds and reptiles. The two main species are the Yellow Mealworm Beetle (pictured below) and the Dark Mealworm Beetle, which has a darker-colored larva, yet the beetle itself is a duller grayish color.

Yellow Mealworm Beetle (left) and its larva (right).

Meal Moths: About 1/2-inch-long, species include the Indian Meal Moth, Angoumois Grain Moth, and Pink Scavenger Caterpillar. All usually lay eggs on the grain and larvae burrow into the kernels. They are prevalent in the Southern USA. Not pictured are the closely-related Mediterranean and European Meal Moths, or the Rice Moth.

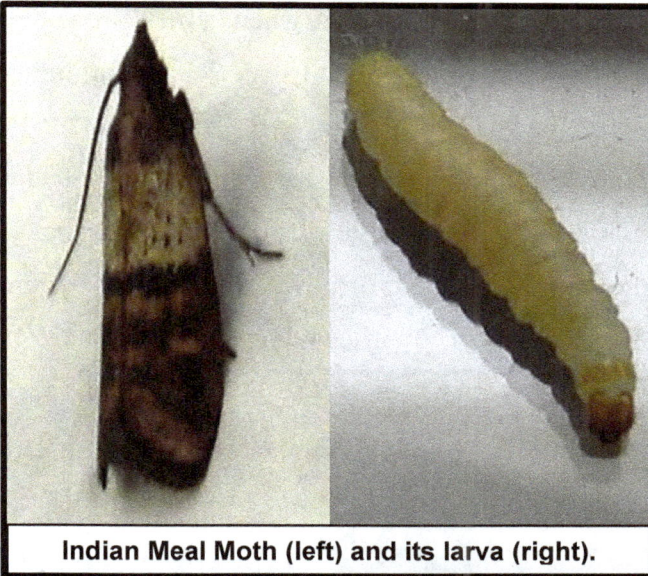

Indian Meal Moth (left) and its larva (right).

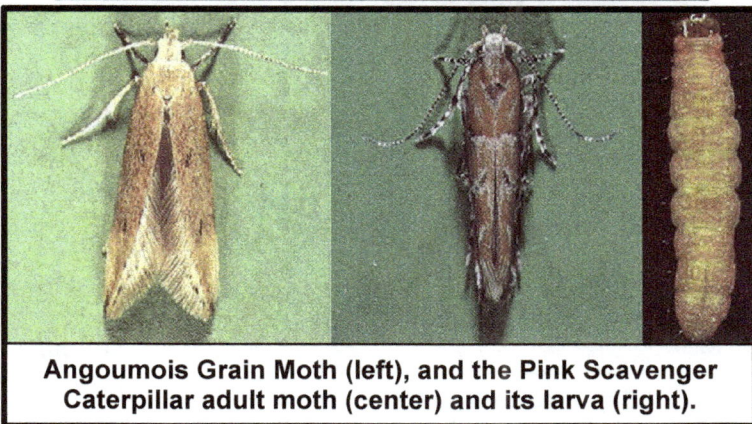

Angoumois Grain Moth (left), and the Pink Scavenger Caterpillar adult moth (center) and its larva (right).

Weevils: Most species are small at about 1/8th -inch-long and have long snouts that can't be mistaken for any other bugs. The only exception is the slightly larger Coffee Bean Weevil, named more for its appearance than its taste in food, and lacks the characteristic snout. Weevils differ in color and markings, but their behavior is the same, most infesting cornfields in the Southern USA when kernels are young and tender. They not only inhabit the fields, but infest the storehouses as well.

There are three very destructive species. The most common is the Maize Weevil, a southern species that chews stored corn into a mound of powder and hulls. The ancient Rice Weevil lives in countries with warmer climates.

The Maize Weevil.

The third species is one of the oldest-known grain pests, called the Granary Weevil, which is a lighter-brown, wingless species that lives mainly in the Northern USA. These three species look very similar to each other.

This Lesser Grain Borer beetle (left) munches on a wheat kernel, and its larva (right).

Grain Borers: These are small but destructive beetles, with jaws strong enough to cut into wood! The tiny (1/8-1/32th of an inch) Lesser Grain Borer is more tropical, and its habitat ranges from Australia to the Gulf States of the USA. It is quite prolific, laying 300-500 eggs in one sitting. Its relatives are the slightly bigger and less destructive Bamboo Powderpost Beetle and the Larger Grain Borer.

Flour Beetles: The Confused Flour Beetle (yes, that is its real name) is only one among many species of Flour Beetles,

Confused Flour Beetle.

which are brown to reddish and about 1/8th inch long. They tend to look relatively similar in appearance, although the Black Flour Beetles look like a miniature version of the Yellow Mealworm Beetle. The most unusual-looking species is the Broadhorned Flour Beetle, that has scary-looking pincer-like protruding jaws. Most Flour Beetles lay eggs in the hundreds and some beetles live up to an entire year! The eggs of the Flat Grain Flour Beetle are so small that laid side by side there would be 150 eggs per inch.

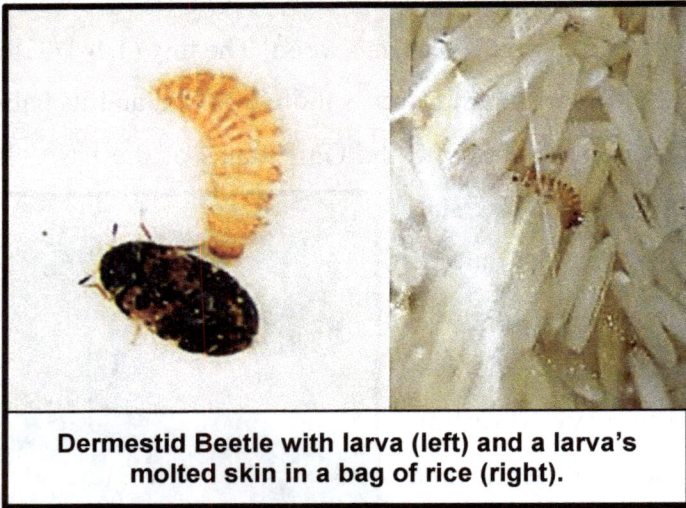

Dermestid Beetle with larva (left) and a larva's molted skin in a bag of rice (right).

Dermestid Beetles: Small at 1/8th-inch or slightly larger, prolific and destructive, these are one of the most commonly found beetles, that feed on anything from flour to skin particles, hence their name of "dermes".

I once found an infestation living in a cat toy made of fur and cork under some furniture, which by the time of discovery, was nothing more than a mound of powder and a clump of hairs! These pests are found just about everywhere, under beds, carpets and in silverware drawers. They can be seen in food clumped together with silk from feeding larvae. Molted skins fly in the air if disturbed, and in the pupal state they look like little hairy balls. Beetles can be very pretty with mottled, multi-colored shells. Depending on the variety, they can have colors of reddish brown, black, tan and gray. Some can live up to several years.

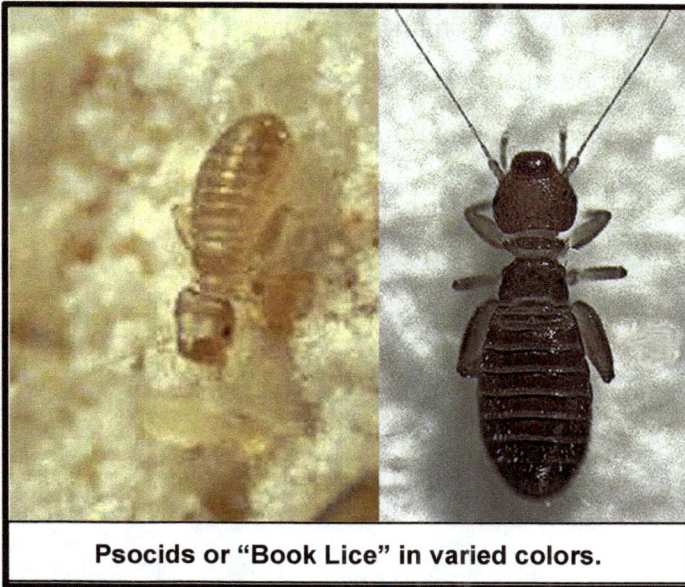

Psocids or "Book Lice" in varied colors.

Psocids: These are also known as "Book Lice", as they can often be found crawling around in books, cardboard and other paper items. They are one of the smallest visible insects at 1/32nd of an inch maximum, and their color ranges anywhere from light white to gray or brown, some being close to transparent. These are perhaps the most prolific and dreaded of all pantry pests, partly because the females can sometimes reproduce asexually. It just takes one!

Now, I always liked bugs as a kid and am not particularly squeamish, but even these things give me the creeps! Given humidity and heat, they can literally cover an area overnight. They are particularly fond of creamy wheat cereals, which when infested, literally appears to be moving. They also tend to like oatmeal, but no grain product is safe when they are present due to their small size. Aside from actually seeing these in food, there's really no other telltale signs that they leave behind. If found in books, it doesn't indicate an infestation. The casual straggler is easily squashed.

Some good examples of bug evidence.
A pupa lies in wait to hatch, surrounded by webs and
stuck-together clumps of powdery food residue.

Chapter 7
"I Like My Noodles Old"
To Publicize or Not

This is perhaps less of an issue than it used to be, due to the growing number of those keeping *yashan*. In communities where few people keep *yashan*, there's a general attitude that one should not make it known that they keep it. Indeed, Rabbi Meir ben Baruch (The Maharam) and Rav Yaakov Kamenetzky kept *yashan* but did not publicize it for that very reason. They urged others to do the same.

Having always lived in smaller Jewish areas, I've known several rabbis who did this. There was a rabbi, (a family friend), who gave that advice to me. He did not keep *yashan*, but had several out-of-town family members who did. He explained that one really shouldn't publicize it, because it seems like one is "boasting". It's as if to say, "I am more religious than you are" to those who don't keep the *mitzvah*. One should never attack another Jew for their *minhag* or beliefs, as long as it is in line with Torah and *Halacha*.

Unless one is invited to dinner and it becomes an issue, there's really no need to talk about it. If you live in an area with a large concentration of Jews where it is commonplace to keep *yashan*, that is a different story. If it's the norm, people talk about it and there's nothing wrong with that.

"In the Home" or "Bring Your Own"

*"**In the Home**"*: In smaller Jewish areas, some have the custom to "only eat *yashan* in their own home". This is most often the case where a person considers keeping *yashan* to merely be a *chumra*, and others around them typically do not keep it. It may also be a case of when a person does not want to publicize that they keep *yashan*, yet they have certain political or social obligations that hinder their observance of the *mitzvah*. In this case, a person might be better off to consider keeping the *mitzvah b'li neder*.

Some people are bothered by the whole concept, as it seems rather like those who "only keep kosher in the home", which is really not keeping kosher at all. In the case of "only keeping *yashan* in the home", unlike with keeping kosher, it has its conditions. First, it only applies in the Diaspora. Second, it only applies to those who see it as a *chumra* and there is nobody else or very few in town who do keep it. Keeping kosher by any means is not "just a *chumra*", so the comparison can sometimes fall short.

*"**Bring your Own**"*: For those of us who do not hold that *yashan* is just a *chumra*, there is another option. If invited out to eat, one can bring their own *yashan* items along.

I was advised by a *rebbetzin* to "BYOB", "bring your own bread" for *Shabbat* dinner wherever I went. This was an excellent piece of advice. In a small town, not only did I have the problem of very few people keeping *yashan*, but being *Sefardi*, I couldn't make *HaMotzi* on the (delicious) sweet *Ashkenazi* challah! Since some people felt bad that they couldn't offer me what I needed, that bit of advice saved me many times. Which brings us to the next topic of discussion, what to do when you eat out at other people's homes.

൞ൽ൞ൽ

Eating Elsewhere

It is never out of fashion to bring along a gift of food, and all the better if it helps out your host! One can refrain from eating any foods that have the Five Grains in them, but sometimes it can be very hard to tell.

There was one Shabbat when literally every single dish my host had was problematic. This was downright embarrassing! It was the height of the *chadash* season, and thankfully, I had at least brought my own challah. However, the salad contained chow mein noodles or the like, the luscious chicken schnitzel (my favorite) was breaded with non-*yashan* bread crumbs, there were two kugels, one made mostly with spaghetti, and the other was of vegetables although it contained flour. So, what was for dessert? A scrumptious-looking apple-strawberry crisp, topped with brown sugar and... you guessed it... oatmeal!

This sort of problem must be dealt with. If you're invited somewhere, treat it like any food allergy. If they know about *yashan*, great! They can determine what you can eat. If they don't even know what *yashan* is, it may be hard to explain, but you can say that you have a dietary restriction called "yashan". With the proliferation of food allergies, hosts often ask if you have any allergies, so this is the perfect time to mention it.

ಬಂತ್ಳಬಂತ್ಳ

Traveling and Keeping Yashan

If one is traveling in the USA from one state to another state, there are many restaurants listed in the end part of the *Guide to Chodosh*. If one knows exactly where they are going, local *kashrut* agencies in the place you are visiting should have a list of restaurants in the area that are *yashan* as well as knowing which stores carry *yashan* foods. In smaller communities where few people keep the *mitzvah*, it's not always publicized if an establishment is *yashan*.

If one is traveling to another country, some places are listed in *Guide to Chodosh*, but it's a good idea to check with *kashrut* agencies in that country. According to some information in the *Guide* and crop reports from the AMIS and USDA on growing seasons in various countries, the next section can help direct you to what local grains are *yashan* in different parts of the world, and what imported products one can rely on. (It doesn't hurt to pack snacks or shelf-stable foods.)

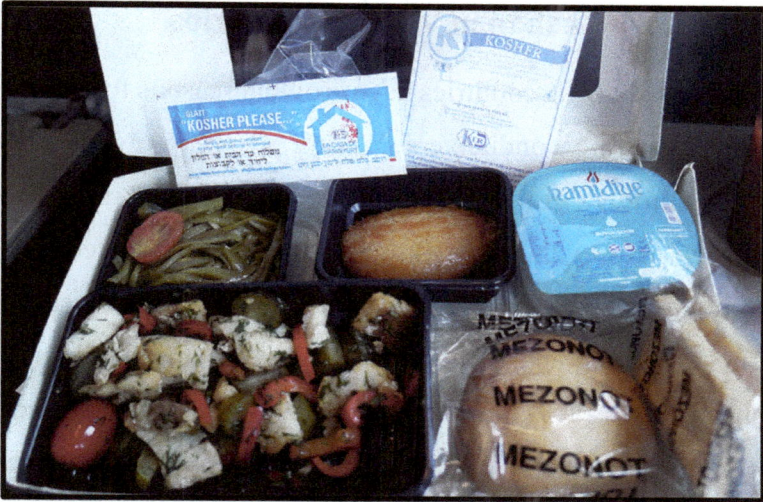

If you are flying, be sure to order a "Special Kosher Meal" from your airline or travel agent, and ask them for it to be *yashan*. In most cases, all frozen Meal Mart dinners and kosher airline caterers should be *yashan*, but not all parts of the meal. Often, there will be a pre-packaged, individual bagel or "Mezonot" roll along with your pre-double-wrapped meal. These may or may not be *yashan*. Then again, if rolls or bagels are being served loose in a basket by the flight attendant, they may not be kosher either!

Most of the time meals should be *yashan*, but always look for a label that says "ישן", "Yoshon" or "Kemach Yashan" to be sure. If you are flying out from Israel, as long as you ordered your "special kosher" meal, it will be *yashan*. No matter where you go, if it's *yashan*, it will be on the label.

133

Yashan in Various Countries

The following countries have growing seasons for certain grains that are conducive for being *yashan*. Any locally-grown product of the grain listed for that country should be *yashan*. However, if there are additional grains mixed with it, it may not be. If one doesn't know if the grain is local or imported, it should be treated as *chadash*. One should still check with a rabbi or the local *kashrut* authority in the area to make sure. Pay close attention to labels and statements from where the grain was grown, not necessarily where it was made. Grains, just like products, can be imported and exported. Imported products must have the date codes checked for their country of origin.

If you find yourself in a different country and do not know for sure what is *yashan* or *chadash*, one can always trust products made in Israel with a reliable *hechsher*. That guarantees it to be *yashan*. Below is grain information on countries around the world, some according to the *Guide* and some from AMIS and the USDA on world crop data.

Africa (North): As with many northern climates, if a product is made with locally-grown barley or winter wheat, it should be *yashan*. If it's not known, treat it as *chadash*. The Equator runs through the exact middle of Africa, so North African seasons are totally the opposite of South African seasons.

Africa (South): Being in the Southern Hemisphere, seasons are reversed from the north, so local wheat and malting barley are *chadash*, since they're planted after *Pesach*. However, the Union of Orthodox Synagogues of South Africa (UOS) covers both Cape Town and Johannesburg, and has regular *Yashan* Bulletins on products. Their web address is: www.uos.co.za. Click on the "Kashrut Information" tab, and at the bottom left, click on the arrow on "Yoshon". Click on the latest date. Note that dates are the opposite of the USA. In Africa (and Canada), they post "yashan dates", where the given date or earlier is *yashan*. To get on their bulletin email list, go to: http://eepurl.com/dccm_H.

Belgium (Antwerp): Locally-grown wheat or barley is *yashan*. Otherwise, treat as *chadash*. If barley is imported from the USA, or wheat flour is blended and not purely from Belgium alone, it could be *chadash*. Some years imported *chadash* barley is used in *cholent*, so make sure you ask about it. This includes local bakeries. Bread and *challot* may be *yashan*. Cakes with yeast are possibly *chadash*.

Canada: Locally-grown winter wheat, spelt or rye it is *yashan*. Barley is usually *chadash*, unless it is marked *yashan*. Often, *chadash* codes are listed by mill codes that are either found within a date code or in the *hechsher* itself. The MK (Montreal Kosher) has *yashan* posts at times. Go to http://mk.ca/news-alerts/ and select "Yoshon Alerts" in the dropdown menu "Browse by Category".

The COR is based in Toronto, but covers all of Canada and has regular bulletins. Their web address is: http://cor.ca/.

To view the bulletin, hover over the "Consumer Resources" tab and go down to "Yoshon Information". Just like Africa, in Canada they post "yashan dates". The given date or earlier is *yashan*. (In the USA, the given date is when it is *chadash*).

China: If a product is made with locally-grown winter wheat, it should be *yashan*. If unknown, treat it as *chadash*.

Egypt: Locally-grown winter wheat should be *yashan*. If it's unknown, treat it as *chadash*.

France: If it is known that a product is made with locally-grown barley or wheat it is probably *yashan*. If it's not known, treat as *chadash*.

Germany: If a product is made with locally-grown wheat or rye it is *yashan*. If it is unknown, treat it as *chadash*.

Hungary: If a product is made with locally-grown wheat, it is most likely *yashan*. If it is not known, treat it as *chadash*.

India: If a product is made with locally-grown winter wheat, it is *yashan*. If unknown, treat it as *chadash*.

Israel: Locally-grown winter wheat is *yashan*. If a product has a reliable Israeli *hechsher*, it is *yashan* anyway. If it is imported from another country, treat it as *chadash*, or look up the date codes from the country of origin if the information is available. Most foods imported from the UK to Israel are *yashan*. Check for reliable *kashrut* symbols in *Yashan Hechsherim*, pages 54-55.

Italy: If it is known that a product is made with locally-grown barley it's *yashan*. Locally-grown "soft wheat" is *yashan*, but durum wheat is *chadash*, therefore since it's difficult to tell, it is better to treat all wheat as *chadash*.

Japan: Locally-grown winter wheat should be *yashan*. If it's unknown, treat it as *chadash*.

Mexico: Locally-grown wheat is always *yashan*. If it is known that a product is made with local wheat, it should be *yashan* as long as there are no other grains mixed in. Mexico is so hot that wheat is only grown there in fall and winter. If it is imported or not known, treat it as *chadash*.

Pakistan: Locally-grown winter wheat should be *yashan*. If it's unknown, treat it as *chadash*.

Poland: Locally-grown wheat or rye is likely to be *yashan*. If it is not known, treat it as *chadash*.

Romania: If a product is made with locally-grown wheat, it should be *yashan*. If it isn't known, treat it as *chadash*.

Spain: Locally-grown barley or wheat is likely *yashan*. Products from imported barley or wheat may be *chadash*.

Sweden: If it is known that a product is made with locally-grown winter wheat, it is *yashan*. If not known, treat it as *chadash*.

Turkey: Local wheat should be *yashan*. If unknown, may be *chadash*.

UK/United Kingdom: All locally-grown wheat or winter barley, is usually *yashan*. Spring wheat is often planted before *Pesach*. If the status is not known or it's imported, it may be *chadash*. The *hashgacha* of Rabbi O. Y. Westheim of Manchester, Kedassia of London, or Rabbi Schneebalg of Edgeware, UK, are all *yashan*. (See page 55 on *Yashan Hechsherim*.) Kedassia can provide *yashan* bulletins for the UK. Email them for more details at: kedassia@kedassia.org.uk.

Ukraine: Locally-grown winter wheat should be *yashan*. If it's unknown, treat it as *chadash*.

USA/United States: If a product is made with locally-grown spelt, rye or winter wheat, it is usually *yashan*. If not known, treat it as *chadash*. Food imported to the USA from most countries should be treated as *chadash*, or look up the date codes from the country it is imported from, if available.

USSR/Former Soviet Union: Locally-grown rye and winter wheat, are *yashan*. If it is not known whether they were grown locally or not, treat it as *chadash*.

Yugoslavia: Locally-grown winter wheat, is *yashan*.

Resources

External Yashan Resources

The following resources can be found online or outside of this book. The organizations, websites, publications and phone hotlines are vital for anyone keeping *yashan*. For those just learning how to keep the *mitzvah*, some other resources include many helpful articles found online.

ೞೞೞೞ

Yashan Organizations

Project Chodosh Inc.: This 501(c)(3) organization publishes the annual *Guide to Chodosh* by Rabbi Yoseph Herman, (the expert on *yashan* in the USA), and has an email list for Bulletin Updates to the *Guide* with corrections and additional products not originally listed. Those on this mailing list can send in an email to receive the *Guide* in digital format by pdf. The mailing list is private, used only by the *Guide to Chodosh* and not given out. They also run a Hotline for questions about products. To donate, make checks payable to *Project Chodosh* and mail to Mrs. C. Rosskamm, 963 Armstrong Ave, Staten Island, NY 10308. Donations are tax-deductible in the USA.

The Yoshon Network Inc.: This 501(c)(3) organization provides the website "Yoshon.com" with most of the information coming from the *Guide to Chodosh*. It provides many resources for those who keep *yashan* or newcomers who want to learn about it, and is geared to help connect and network people around the world. The website and all operations are supported entirely by donations and is volunteer only. To donate, go to Yoshon.com and click on the PayPal button. Donations are tax-deductible in the USA.

ৰা৩৪ৰা৩

Yashan Publications

"A Guide to Chodosh" by Rabbi Yoseph Herman: The only publication of its kind, this is a "must have" for anyone keeping *yashan*. This is the authority on products, restaurants, caterers and wholesalers in the USA, and has information on some items from other countries. The *Guide* is produced by Project Chodosh Inc. One can order a printed copy of the *Guide*, called a subscription. There's a *Preliminary Guide* and the final *Guide* usually comes out after *Sukkot*. One can buy a printed copy of the *Guide* in various locations by calling their hotline. The various ways to receive a copy are on page 142.

ৰা৩৪ৰা৩

Yashan Phone Hotlines for Product Questions

Project Chodosh Hotline: Rabbi Herman's Project Chodosh has a "Chodosh Hotline", where people can ask questions and they are answered via recorded message. The Chodosh

Hotline is available 24 hours a day (located in Eastern Time). Their number is (718) 305-5133. It features a complex phone menu, and questions asked throughout the week are answered on certain days, each day having a number. One can also order printed copies of the *Guide* on the Hotline.

ᏚᏣᎦᏚᏣᎦ
Yashan Product Information Websites

Yoshon.com: Yoshon.com is a website devoted entirely to keeping *yashan*, and is the only website of its kind. It is run by The Yoshon Network Inc. The site is based mainly on the information found in *Guide to Chodosh*.

Its main function is reporting the *yashan* status and date codes of products (but not caterers or restaurants). Each entry shows a picture of the item, a list of similar products, all grain ingredients, the *hechsher*, any *yashan hashgacha*, and other information a *yashan*-keeping consumer may need. It's mobile-friendly, and a product's status can be looked up instantly as one is shopping in the grocery store.

It offers articles for newcomers, lists contacts around the world, has an instructions page on the Chodosh Hotline, and a detailed download page to get the *Guide to Chodosh*, Bulletin Updates, South African, British and Canadian *yashan* reports, among other things. There is a Yoshon.com App planned for the future. The web address is: https://Yoshon.com.

Guides, Bulletins and Email Lists

A Guide to Chodosh: To get a free pdf version, email chodosh@moruda.com, or chodosh@sefer.org, and be sure there's something in the subject and body. For a printed copy, the cost (as of this printing) is $18 within the USA, $20 to Canada or Mexico, and $25 for Israel or other countries. Call 646-278-1189 to record credit card number and address, or write your full name, address, home phone number, credit card number credit card expiration date on paper, and fax it to 888-755-7590. Checks aren't recommended.

ഇൻലൈ ഇൻലൈ

Yashan Bulletins, Updates and Email Lists

Chodosh Bulletin Updates: Corrections and additions to the *Guide.* To be added, email: chodosh-subscribe@lists.projectgenesis.org.

Kashruth Council of Canada (COR) Canadian Yoshon Updates: To view, go to: www.cor.ca, click on "Consumer Resources", and go down to "Yoshon Information". For *yashan* email updates, send an email to Rabbi Heber at: theber@cor.ca.

Kemach Food Products Corp.: Kemach's page for status of their *yashan* products: http://www.kemach.com/yoshon.html For their updates, send an email to: yoshon@kemach.com.

Kedassia Yoshon Updates: For the UK: kedassia@kedassia.org.uk.

MK Yoshon Updates: For Canada's Montreal Kosher list of products and establishments, go to: http://mk.ca/news-alerts/, and in the "Browse by Category" menu, go to "Yoshon". Click on "Search" for updates. To get on their list, email: info@mk.ca.

Star-K "Yoshon Quick Reference Guide": Star-K of Baltimore has a mini version of the *Guide* for download, featuring products and local Baltimore establishments. Click on "Quick Reference Guide", the link to the latest download: http://www.star-k.org/articles/category/yoshon/

Union of Orthodox Synagogues of South Africa Yoshon Updates: To view "Update Notices" go to: http://www.uos.co.za/kashrut/ and click on "Yoshon" on the menu to the left at the bottom, and all the titles come up. Click on the latest title to view current *yashan* report. To receive their email updates, go to: http://eepurl.com/dccm_H.

Yoshon.com Newsletter and News Alerts: To subscribe to the monthly newsletter and instant email alerts featuring news, updates and recalls on *yashan* products, go to: https://Yoshon.com, and click on the newsletter link to subscribe.

৪০ল৪০ল

Online Audio/Videos About Yashan

"Yoshon Basics", 9/19/16, "cRc" video on how to use the *Guide*: https://www.youtube.com/watch?v=rTvkdObUEdM The same class is in audio from "YU Torah": http://www.yutorah.org/lectures/lecture.cfm/861179/rabbi-dovid-cohen-crc-/yoshon-basics-basics-guide-to-chodosh-details-yoshon-in-chicago/

Online Articles About Yashan

Note: More articles can be found in the Bibliography.

"*'Beer Halacha': Clarifying the Kashrus of Beer*" by: Rabbi Tzvi Rosen, Published in the Winter Kashrus Kurrents 2014: https://www.star-k.org/articles/kashrus-kurrents/2183/beer-halacha-clarifying-the-kashrus-of-beer/

"*Going With the Grain*" by Rabbi Yosef Dovid Chanowitz from "Kosher Spirit". Excellent article on *yashan* and grain products: www.ok.org/kosherspirit/fall-2008/going-with-the-grain/

"*Kosher Spirit*" *Online Magazine from OK, Winter Wheat Questions and Yashan*". Interesting Q & A about *yashan*: www.ok.org/kosherspirit/winter-2009/share-your-spirit-5/

"*Out with the Old, In with the New - The Laws of Chodosh*" 2004. Rabbi Aaron Ross from Chabura-Net. Wonderfully thorough article on yashan and its history concerning rabbinic views. http://www.chaburas.org/chodosh.html

"*Preparing For Yoshon: Practically Speaking, A Housewife's Perspective On Keeping Yoshon*" www.star-k.org/articles/articles/seasonal/442/preparing-for-yoshon-practically-speaking-a-housewifes-perspective-on/

"*What is "Yashan?*" by Menachem Posner. A Chabad rabbi in Scotland, tells of reasons for *yashan* leniencies:: http://www.chabadofedinburgh.com/library/article_cdo/aid/584873/jewish/What-is-Yashan.htm

"*Yoshon*". Discussions and *Halachic* sources:
https://oukosher.org/blog/consumer-kosher/yoshon/

"*Yoshon and Chodosh Something Old and Something New*":
http://www.star-k.org/articles/articles/seasonal/436/yoshon-and-chodosh-something-old-and-something-new/

"*Yoshon: Frequently Asked Questions*". Various questions asked to Canada's COR rabbis from beginner to advanced:
http://www.cor.ca/view/499/yoshon_frequently_asked_quetions.html
(Note: The above address is not a typo.)

"*Yoshon and Chodosh*", February 15, 2008. Article with some mention of keeping *yashan* in Israel:
http://www.jerusalemkoshernews.com/2008/02/yoshon-and-chodosh/

ಬಂಗಬಂಗ

Online Sources for Buying Yashan Foods

For those of us who don't live in large Jewish areas, the following are some online resources for buying *yashan* foods:

In Most Countries

Ships internationally, and to the USA, UK and Ireland, France, Canada, Germany, Italy, Spain, Netherlands, Australia, Brazil, Japan, China, India, and Mexico: (*Use proper country suffix.) https://www.amazon.*

In Europe

Kosher 4 U (Delivers all over Europe, the UK and Ireland):
https://www.kosher4u.eu/

In the USA

The following sites ship anywhere within the Continental USA. Some may include Canada, Alaska, Hawaii, and Puerto Rico. Check the sites to be sure before ordering if you live there. At the time of printing, the following charges apply to these sites.

No Minimum Orders:

Makolet Online:
https://www.makoletonline.com/

My Kosher Market:
https://www.mykoshermarket.com/

Park East Kosher:
https://www.parkeastkosher.com/

Free Shipping with $100 Orders

AviGlatt ($100 or more is free shipping):
https://www.aviglatt.com/

The Gluten-Free Shoppe ($100 or more is free shipping):
http://www.theglutenfreeshoppe.com/

Minimum Orders

Rockland Kosher ($40 minimum order):
https://rocklandkosher.com/

Glatt Kosher Store ($100 minimum order):
https://www.glattkosherstore.com/

Vintage Grain Reference Resources

These are resources within this book for newcomers or seasoned *yashan*-keepers alike, including Hebrew terms on packages, a Glossary, and answers to the *Date Codes* Quiz.

ഇ൦ഌഇ൦ഌ

Hebrew and Terms on Food Packages

Below are common words and terms found on kosher food packaging. (*Ashkenazic* pronunciation is in italics.)

בשר = **Basar:** "Meat".

בית יוסף = **Bet Yosef/*Beys Yoseif*:** (See "*Chalak Bet Yosef*".) Beef lungs are totally free of adhesions.

בהשגחת =**B'hashgachat ... /*B'hashgachas* ... :** "Under the supervision of…" {name of Rabbi in charge}.

בישול ישראל = **Bishul Yisrael/*Bishul Yisroel*:** "Cooked by a Jew".

ברכתו מזונות = **Birchato Mezonot/*Birchoso Mezonos*:** "Its blessing is '*Mezonot*'". (Dough w/ juice.)

חלב = **Chalav/*Cholov*:** "Dairy".

חלבי= **Chalavi/*Cholovi*.** "Dairy".

חלב ישראל = **Chalav Yisrael/*Cholov Yisroel*:** "Dairy product constantly supervised by a Jew".

חלק בית יוסף = **Chalak Bet Yosef/*Chalak Beis Yoseif*:** "'Smooth' as by Rabbi Yosef Cairo" (for beef lungs).

חמץ = **Chametz/*Chometz*:** "Leavening". (Not for *Pesach*.)

גלאט כשר = ***Glatt Kosher*:** "Smooth". Kosher beef having had the lungs checked.

כשר בשר = **Kasher Basar/*Kosher Basar*:** "Kosher Meat".

כשר = **Kasher/*Kosher*:** "Fit for Jewish consumption".

כשר חלב ישראל = **Kasher, Chalav Yisrael/*Kosher, Cholov Yisroel*:** (See "*Chalav Yisrael*".)

כשר למהדרין= **Kasher L'Mehadrin/*Kosher L'Mehadrin*:** "Kosher of extra-fine quality".

כשר לפסח = **Kasher L'Pesach/*Kosher L'Peysach*:** "Kosher for *Pesach*". Fit for Passover use.

כשר פארווע = **Kasher, Parve/*Kosher, Pareve*.** "Kosher Neutral", neither dairy or meat

קמח ישן = **Kemach Yashan/*Yoshon*:** "*Yashan* Flour".

נעשה מקמח ישן = **Na'aseh M'Kemach Yashan/*Na'aseh M'Kemach Yoshon*.** "Made of *Yashan* flour".

פארווע = **Parve or Pareve.** "Neutral", neither dairy or meat.

פת ישראל = **Pat Yisrael/*Pas Yisroel*:** "Baked by a Jew".

ישן = **Yashan/ *Yoshon*:** "*Yashan*", literally "old" grain.

148

Glossary of Hebrew

Below is a list of Hebrew words and phrases to help newcomers become familiar with them.

Pronunciations: All stressed syllables are in bold. Most words used in this book are in the common form of *Sefardic* Hebrew (modern Israeli Hebrew). *Ashkenazic* spellings and pronunciations (appearing in *Guide to Chodosh*) are in italics. Similar pronunciations aren't distinguished.

"Ch" is listed for the Hebrew letters "Chet" and "Chaf", a sound rather like one clearing their throat.

Anavim: (**Ah**-nah-**veem**) Grapes.

Arlah: (Ahr-**lah**) *(Ohr-lah)* Fruit from a tree in its first three years, which is sacred.

Ashkenazi: (Ash-**ken**-ah-**zee**) *(Ash-ken-aw-zee)* Literally "Ashkenazite". A European Jew.

Ashkenazic: Pertaining to Jews of European descent.

Ashkenazim: (Ash-**ken**-ah-**zeem**) *(Ash-ken-aw-zim)* Jews of European descent. There are many different branches, such as Russian, Polish, German, Litvak (Lithuanian).

Bal Tashchit: (Ball tah-**shkheet**) The *mitzvah* of not wasting, especially food; derived from not cutting down fruit trees in times of war in *Devarim* 20:19-20.

Bamidbar: (**Bah**-meed-**bar**) *(Bah-**mid**-bar)* The Book of Numbers. Literally "in the desert" or "in the wilderness".

Bereshit: (**Beh**-reh-**sheet** or Breh-**sheet**) *(**Brey**-shees)* The Book of Genesis.

Birkat HaMazon: (Beer-**kaht Hah**-Mah-**zon**) Literally "Blessing for the food". A prayer said after eating bread.

B'li Neder: (Be-**lee Neh**-der) Without a vow.

Bracha/*Brocho*: (Brah-**chah**) *(**Bro**-chah)* Blessing. Also written "b'racha", "berachah" or "bracha".

Brachot/*Brochos*: (Brah-**chot**) *(**Bro**-chos)* Blessings. Also written "b'rachot" or "berachot".

Chadash/Chodosh: (Chah-**dahsh**) *(**Chaw**-dawsh)* New. Refers mainly to forbidden spring grain.

Challah: (Chah-**lah**) *(**Chah**-lah)* Traditional bread named for the tithe taken from dough. *Challah* is a type of tithe meant for only *Kohanim*.

Chameshet Minei Dagan: (Cha-**meh**-shet Mee-**nei** Dah-**gahn**) *(Chaw-**meh**-shes Mih-nei Daw-**gawn**)* The Five Species of Grain, Wheat, Barley, Oats, Rye, and Spelt.

Chametz/*Chometz*: (Chah-**metz**) *(**Cho**-metz)* Leavening.

Chassidim: (**Cha**-see-**deem**) *(Cha-**sih**-dim)* "Ultra-Orthodox" *Ashkenazic* Jews, often of Polish or

Ukrainian descent. Groups include Breslover, Bubover, Lubavitch and Satmar, each following their specific *rebbe*. They follow teachings of the Ba'al Shem Tov.

Chittim: (Chee-**teem**) Wheat.

Chol HaMoed: (Chol Ha-**Mo**-ed) Middle days of the holidays of *Sukkot* and *Pesach*.

Chumrah: (Choom-**rah**) *(Chum-rah)* An extra stringency that not everyone practices.

Chumrot: (Choom-**rot**) *(Chum-ros)* Extra stringencies.

Devarim: (**Dev**-ah-**reem**) *(Deh-vah-reem)* The book of Deuteronomy; Literally meaning "words".

Gemara: (**Geh**-mar-**ah**) *(Geh-mo-rah)* Section of *Talmud* written by later rabbis, expounding on the *Mishneh*.

Halachah: (**Ha**-lah-**chah**) *(Ha-lo-chah)* Torah Law.

Halachot: (**Ha**-lah-**chot**) *(Ha-law-chos)* Torah Laws.

HaMotzi: (**Ha**-Mo-**tzee**) *(Ha-Motz-ee)* Blessing made on bread after the hand-washing.

Hashgacha/*Hashgocho*: (**Hahsh**-go-**chah**) Kosher or *yashan* supervision.

Hechsher: (**Hech**-sher) A *kashrut* supervising agency's or organization's certification or "seal of approval".

Hechsherim: (**Hech**-sher-**eem**) *(Hech-sher-im)* Plural of *hechsher*.

Kasher: (Kah-**sher**) 1. (Adverb) Literally "fit". (The proper Israeli Hebrew pronunciation of "kosher".)

(**Kah**-sher) 2. (Verb) To make fit for use or consumption.

For Meat: Procedure to remove excess blood.

For Cookware: To make kosher by a specific procedure.

Kashrut: (Ka-**shroot**) *(Kawsh-roos)* "Fitness of". Referring to the Jewish dietary laws.

Kohanim: (**Ko**-ha-**neem**) *(Ko-hah-nim)* Aaron's offspring designated to be Temple priests.

Kohen: (Ko-**hen**) *(Ko-heyn)* A descendent of Aaron, designated to give the priestly blessing.

Kosher: (*Ko-sher*) Fit for consumption. (This is actually the *Ashkenazic* pronunciation of "*kasher*", which has made its way into popular English as meaning "proper".)

Kusemet: (Koo-**seh**-met**)** : *(Koo-seh-mes)* Spelt (also sometimes called "Kusmin").

Kusmin: (Koos-**meen**) : *(Koos-min)* Spelt (also sometimes called "Kusemet").

Ma'aser: (**Ma**'-ah-**sehr**) *(Mah-ser)* Tithe.

Masechet: (Mah-**seh**-chet) *(Mah-seh-ches)* A Tractate of the *Talmud*.

Mashgiach: (Mash-**gee**-ach) Kosher supervisor. (Plural are Masgichim; A female supervisor is a *Mashgichah*.)

Matzah: (Mah-**tzah**) *(Mahtz-ah* or *Mahtz-oh)* Unleavened bread, known for being eaten on Passover. (Plural is *Matzot*.)

Me'ein Shalosh: (Meh-'**eyn** Shah-**losh**) Literally "three condensed". "Title" of blessing said after eating certain grain snacks, wine, grape juice, and certain fruits, named for the three main *blessings* of *Birkat HaMazon*, which are condensed into one blessing.

Mesorah: (**Meh**-so-**rah**) *(Meh-so-rah)* Tradition passed down from parent to child from their country of origin.

Mezonot: (**Meh**-zo-**not**) *(Muh-zo-nos)* The blessing said before eating any product made of the Five Grains.

Minhag: (Meen-**hag**) *(Min-hawg)* A custom.

Minhagim: (Meen-ha-**geem**) *(Min-haw-gim)* Customs.

Mishnah: (Meesh-**nah**) *(Mish-nah)* Part of the Talmud or Oral Tradition written down by the early Rabbis.

Mitzvah: (Meetz-**vah**) *(Mitz-vah)* Usually, one of 613 Torah laws. Also can mean a good deed.

Mitzvot: (Meetz-**vot**) *(Mitz-vos)* Plural of mitzvah.

Omer: (**Oh**-mehr) The Barley Offering in Temple times.

Orlah: (Ahr-**lah**) *(Ohr-lah)* Fruit of a tree in its first 3 years.

Pesach: (**Peh**-sach) *(Pey-sach)* The major holiday of Passover.

P'sak: (P-**sak**) A *Halachic* ruling or judgement.

Rimmon: (Ree-**mohn**) Pomegranate.

Rishonim: (**Ree**-sho-**neem**) *(Ree-**sho**-nim)* Earlier Rabbis.

Rosh Hashanah: (Rosh Hah—shah-**nah**) *(Rosh Hah— shah-nah)* Literally, "head of the year".

Sefardi: (**Seh**-far-**dee** or Sfar-**dee**) *(**Sfar**-di)* Literally "Sefardite". A *Sefardic* Jew. See *Sefardim*.

Sefardim: (**Seh**-far-**deem** or Seh-**fahr**-ah-**deem**) *(Seh-**far**-dim or **Sfar**-dim)* Jews of Spanish, Asian, African or Middle Eastern descent, from the Hebrew word for Spain "Sefarad".

Se'orim: (**Seh**-'or-**eem**) Barley.

Shavu'ot: (**Shah**-voo-'ot) *(Shah-**voo**-us)* Literally "weeks". Major holiday 7 weeks after Passover.

Shemot: (Sheh-**mot**) *(Sheh-**mos**)* The Book of Exodus. Literally "Names".

Shibbolet Shual: (Shee-**bo**-let Shoo-'**al**) *(Shee-**bow**-les Shoo-wal)* Oats.

Shifon: (Shee-**fohn**) Rye.

Sh'mittah: (She-mee-**tah**) *(**Shmee**-tah)* The seventh year ordained for the land to rest in the agricultural cycle of Israel.

Talmud: (Tal-**mood**) *(Tal-mud)* The Oral Tradition, written down in book form.

Tamar: (Tah-**mar**) Date or date palm.

Te'enah: (Teh-ʻ**en**-ah) Figs.

Terumah: (**Teh**-roo-**mah**) *(Teh-**roo**-mah)* Specific tithe always given to *Kohanim*. *Challah* is a type of *terumah*.

Vayikra: (**Vah**-yeek-**rah**) *(Vai-**yeek**-rah)* The Book of *Leviticus*. Literally, "He called out".

Yashan/*Yoshon*: (Ya-**shan**) *(Yaw-shen)* "Old". Pertains to "old" grain. Sometimes listed as "*yoshon*" on products.

Yisrael: (**Yees**-rah-**ehl**) *(Yis-roh-eyl)* Israel.

Zayit: (Zah-**yeet**) *(Zai-yis)* Olive.

ꙮꙊꙮꙊ

Answers to the Date Code Quiz

On the following two pages are the answers to the "Test Your Knowledge of Date Codes" Quiz. (The original quiz can be found in Chapter 5 on pages 104-106.)

1. **No, it is *chadash*.** Why? The Julian date is three days after the *chadash* cut-off date.

2. **Yes, it is *yashan*.** Why? The date is earlier than the date listed in the *Guide*. Since the Guide doesn't mention it, we ignore the general cut-off dates, since this company may have different grain sources and may have a later packing date.

3. **Yes, it is *yashan*.** Why? The date is earlier than the *Guide's*. Knowing the ingredients isn't crucial, especially for barley, which it doesn't even contain. It has malt!

4. **No, it is *chadash*.** Why? The date is later than the *Guide's*. Ignore ingredients, it has the date code.

5. **Yes, it is *yashan*.** Why? Regardless of the year, your Julian date is earlier than the date in the *Guide*.

6. For the *Guide* in the USA- **No, it's *chadash*.** Why? It is the actual "*chadash* date", and needs to be *before* the date to be *yashan*. If you live anywhere else in the world- **Yes, it's *yashan*.** Why? Other countries report the "*yashan* date", so the reported date to be *yashan* is that date or earlier.

7. **Yes, it is *yashan*.** Why? Just because July 31, is 212, on the Julian calendar it means nothing because the *Guide* says to ignore the "best by date". The LOT number is the important item, and your package says the lot number 7197 is before the *Guide's* 7211.

8. **No, it is *chadash*.** Why? Oats are *chadash* earlier than wheat, and the oat date in the *Guide's* "Shaker Chart" is before the date on the Fun Flakes box.

9. **Yes, it is *yashan*.** Why? The wheat date on the box is earlier than in the *Guide's* "Shaker Chart".

10. **Yes, it is *yashan*.** Why? The oat date on the box is earlier than in the *Guide's* "Shaker Chart".

Bibliography

Compilation of sources used for information or images that helped in the creation of *Vintage Grain*, includes many wonderful articles on *yashan*, both online and in print.

Books and Publications:

The Artscroll Series/Stone Edition. *The Chumash.* Brooklyn: Mesorah Publications, Ltd., 1998, 2000.

Blumenkrantz, Rabbi Avrohom. *The Laws of Pesach: A Digest.* Far Rockaway: Gross Bros. Printing Co. Inc., 5764-2004 Edition, published annually.

Capone, Deirdre Marie. *Uncle Al Capone: The Untold Story from Inside His Family.* Bonita Springs: Recap Publishing, 2012.

Chafetz Chayim, Translated by Charles Wengrov. *The Concise Book of Mitzvoth: The Commandments Which Can Be Observed Today.* (*Mitzvot* 101-103). Jerusalem, Israel: Feldheim Publishers, January 1, 1990.

Esterow, Milton. *Matriarch Keeps Rein on Business: Regina Margareten at 95 Is Still the Boss at Kosher Food Products Concern.* New York Times, December 24, 1957.

Herman, Rabbi Yoseph (Assisted by Chaya Rosskamm). *A Guide to Chodosh.* Kew Gardens: Project Chodosh, 5776-2016 Edition, published annually.

Prial, Frank J. *Wine Talk* .The New York Times, April 6, 1974.

Sarna, Jonathan D. *How Matzah Became Square: Manischewitz and the Development of Machine-Made Matzah in the United States.* Touro College, Graduate School of Jewish Studies, 2005.

Sears, David. *The Path of the Baal Shem Tov: Early Chasidic Teachings and Customs.* Lanham: Rowman and Littlefield Publishers, Inc., October 1996.

Wrigley, Colin W., Harold Corke, Koushik Seetharaman, and Jonathan Faubion. *Encyclopedia of Food Grains.* Kidlington, Oxford, UK: Academic Press, 2004, 2015.

ॐ൬ॐ൬

Online Articles and Reference Websites

Agricultural Market Information System (AMIS) Crop Calendars. (Published semi-annually) http://www.amis-outlook.org/fileadmin/user_upload/amis/docs/Crop_Calendar/AMIS_Crop_Calendar.pdf

Aish.com Staff. "613 Commandments". (Article including Mitzvot 197-199.) Published January 13, 2002. http://www.aish.com/h/sh/se/48945081.html

Canadian Grain Commission (Government of Canada). "Identify An Insect". (Online reference for grain producers). https://www.grainscanada.gc.ca/storage-entrepose/ipi-iir-eng.htm

DIN Ask the Rabbi, Halacha Talk. "The Prohibition of Chodosh". March 28, 2012.
http://dinonline.org/2012/03/28/the-prohibition-of-chodosh/

Eveleth, Rose. Smithsonian.com. "'Sell By' And 'Best By' Dates on Food Are Basically Made Up-But Hard to Get Rid Of". March 28, 2014.
http://www.smithsonianmag.com/smart-news/sell-and-best-dates-food-are-basically-made-hard-get-rid-180950304/

Food Timeline. "FAQs: Cakes", source for much on cake mixes. Last modified January 23, 2015.
http://www.foodtimeline.org/foodcakes.html

"Gallery of Graphic Design", source for many vintage advertisements. Last accessed July 23, 2017.
http://graphic-design.tjs-labs.com/

Gorelik, Rabbi David. Rabbinical Coordinator, OU Kosher. "Yoshon". October 8, 2015.
https://oukosher.org/blog/consumer-kosher/yoshon/

Gorelik, Rabbi David. Rabbinical Coordinator, OU Kosher. "Yoshon in America 5768". Daf HaKashrus, Dec. 2007.
https://oukosher.org/content/uploads/2013/02/Daf_16-3.pdf

H. J. Heinz Company. "57 Exposition Number". 1909. (Alaska-Yukon-Pacific Exposition Digital Collection: Seattle Public Library).
http://cdm200301.cdmhost.com/cdm/compoundobject/collection/p200301coll1/id/2084/rec/79

Institute of Food Technologists Journal. "Comprehensive Reviews in Food Science and Food Safety". "Applications and Perceptions of Date Labeling of Food" Vol. 13, Issue 4. June 21, 2014. http://onlinelibrary.wiley.com/doi/10.1111/1541-4337.12086/full

Kaginoff, Rabbi Yirmiyohu. "Chodosh in Chul". November 1, 2010. http://www.jerusalemkoshernews.com/2010/11/chodosh-in-chul/

The Kosher Food Distributors Association in Conjunction with Integrated Marketing Communications. "The History of Kosher Food in the USA". Revised January, 2000. http://boards.fool.com/history-of-kosher-food-in-us-long-19316780.aspx?sort=threaded

Linzer, Rabbi Dov. YC Torah Library. "Mesechet Menachot: The Taxonomy of the Gemara's Grains", contradictory source on grains not originating in the Fertile Crescent. Posted on May 20, 2011. https://library.yctorah.org/2011/05/mesechet-menachot-the-taxonomy-of-the-gemaras-grains/

Lubinsky, Menachem. "Kosher Living article, The Changing Kosher Airline Meals Scene". Jewish World Review. June 21 1999. www.jewishworldreview.com/kosher/living062199.asp

Marcus, Shmuel. "The Indomitable Spirit of Rabbi Ahron Soloveichik" Jewish Action Magazine, OU Kosher. October 13, 2002. https://www.ou.org/jewish_action/10/2002/indomitable-spirit-rabbi-ahron-soloveichik/

Medoff, Rafael. "The Orthodox Union's Early Years: Fighting for Jewish Rights in a Very Different America". Jewish Action Magazine, OU Kosher. March 18, 2016. https://www.ou.org/jewish_action/03/2016/the-orthodox-unions-early-years-fighting-for-jewish-rights-in-a-very-different-america/

Moore, Mario. Harvard University. "Food Labeling Regulation: A Historical and Comparative Survey 2001". http://nrs.harvard.edu/urn-3:HUL.InstRepos:8965597

National Frozen and Refrigerated Foods Association, Inc. Consumer Articles. "History of Frozen Foods is Long and Varied". May 14, 2009. https://www.nfraweb.org/resources/articles/details.aspx?ArticleId=18

OK Laboratories. "Timeline of Kosher". Last accessed June 28, 2017. www.ok.org/about/our-ongoing-story/a-timeline-of-kosher/

Park, Michael Y., BonAppetit.com. "A History of the Cake Mix, the Invention That Redefined 'Baking'". September 26, 2013. https://www.bonappetit.com/entertaining-style/pop-culture/article/cake-mix-history

Spitz, Rabbi Yehuda. 3-Part Article from Ohr Someach, "Chodosh in Chutz L'Aretz". January 14, 2012. https://ohr.edu/4991

Tannenbaum, Rabbi Gershon. "A Call For Increased Kosher Law Enforcement". January 7, 2016. http://matzav.com/a-call-for-increased-kosher-law-enforcement/

United States Department of Agriculture. "Food Product Dating". Dec 14, 2016.
https://www.fsis.usda.gov/wps/portal/fsis/topics/food-safety-education/get-answers/food-safety-fact-sheets/food-labeling/food-product-dating/food-product-dating

United States Department of Agriculture. "Stored Grain Insect Reference". September 2016.
https://www.gipsa.usda.gov/fgis/publication/ref/Stored%20Grain%20Insects_2015-03-04.pdf

United States Department of Agriculture. "Major World Crop Areas and Climatic Profiles". Revised September 1994.
http://usda.mannlib.cornell.edu/usda/nass/general/ah/ah664.pdf

"Yalkut Yosef". *Halacha* 11, source for Quote from Rav Ovadia Yosef. April 26, 2014.
http://www.yalkut.info/category/הלכות-מזוזה-ומעקה/

Yeshivaworld.com. "Yoshon on the Rise: The Kof-K and ConAgra Foods; New Joint Venture to Make Old Product". August 10, 2009.
http://www.theyeshivaworld.com/news/general/38064/yoshon-on-the-rise-the-kof-k-and-conagra-foods-new-joint-venture-to-make-old-product.html

Index

(All page numbers for pictures are in italics.)

A

B

C

V

W

Y

About the Author:

Chasya Katriela Eshkol is the Executive Director and founder of The Yoshon Network Inc., a 501 (c)(3) non-profit organization dedicated solely to the *mitzvah* of keeping *yashan*. TYNI was organized in Cincinnati, Ohio, where she initiated the start of the once rather humble beginnings of the Yoshon.com website. Since then, she married Shmaryahu Jaim Eshkol and moved to Scottsdale, Arizona, where the TYNI base-of-operations is currently located. Her husband, runs a web agency "Tovim Media, LLC", and redesigned Yoshon.com, turning it into an easy-to-use, searchable and responsive site. TYNI continues to grow and expand, helping to provide *yashan* information to visitors all over the world.

Chasya has written articles for *Jewish Spirit Magazine* for the Cincinnati Community Kollel, created articles and poetry for the *Cincinnati Jewish Women's Journal,* pen and ink drawings, the *Pet Pride Inc.* newsletter, and previously created word and crossword puzzles for *The Morris Report* published by Alexander Auerbach and Co. She is the author of *Can-Do Kosher! A Quick and Concise Guide to Becoming Kosher*, and is finishing up another large book project started in 2005, which should be completed sometime in 2019.

Chasya can be reached at WriteChasya@gmail.com.

Tovim Press

book publishing services that are simply, Tov!

Quality Books Published by Tovim Press, LLC.

Scan the QR code above or visit us at TovimPress.com,

for book publishing services that are simply, Tov!

www.ingramcontent.com/pod-product-compliance
Lightning Source LLC
Chambersburg PA
CBHW070931030426
42336CB00014BA/2623